A Dad's Toolbox for Better Parenting

A DAD'S TOOLBOX
FOR BETTER PARENTING

by
Dave Kovar

A Dad's Toolbox for Better Parenting
by Dave Kovar

Copyright © 2011 Dave Kovar, Carmichael, California
All Rights Reserved

NOTICE OF RIGHTS
No part of this publication may be reproduced, stored in or introduced into a retrieval system, or transmitted in any form or by any means (electronic, mechanical, photocopying, recording, scanning or otherwise) without the prior written permission of the author or publisher.

First Paperback Edition 24 Feb. 2011
Manufactured in the United States of America

The author acknowledges the trademarked status and trademark owners of the following wordmarks mentioned in this work:

- Frisbee: Wham-O Mfg. Co.
- Indiana Jones: Lucasfilm Ltd.
- Cheetos: Frito-Lay North America Inc.
- Grapenuts: POST® Natural Cereals
- Popsicle Unilever United States
- Twinkies: Hostess Brands, Inc.
- Lucky Charms: General Mills
- V-8: CSC Brands LP
- The Biggest Loser

ISBN: 978-1-4611-0622-7
Library of Congress Control Number: 2011921861

Dedication

It really does take an entire village to "raise a book."

To my mom, dad, brother Tim and sister Cindy, all of whom are great parenting role models ... to my amazing team of instructors, students and their parents from whom I have learned so much over the years ... to my beautiful wife, Angelina, for her undying support ... and to my son, Alex, and daughter, Melissa, who have been wonderful teachers.

A special thanks to Jennifer Ann Gordon for her creative input and tireless effort, to Dave Chamberlain for his gentle push to get A DAD'S TOOLBOX FOR BETTER PARENTING completed ... and to Brian Kendall for his artistic touches.

Table of Contents

FOREWORD	XIII
ABOUT THE AUTHOR	XVII
INTRODUCTION	XXI
SECTION 1: PARENTING BASICS	**23**

Guideline 1: Praise in public, but reprimand in private 26

Guideline 2: Believe in your child's potential 30

Guideline 3: Walk your talk 34

Guideline 4: Constantly catch your child "doing things right" 38

Guideline 5: Set boundaries and stick to them 42

Guideline 6: Listen 46

Guideline 7: Hold your child to a high standard 50

Guideline 8: Inspire your child to greatness 54

Guideline 9: Choose your battles 58

Guideline 10: Be easily in awe 62

Guideline 11: Give your child choices, not ultimatums 66

Guideline 12: Never compare 70

Guideline 13: Maintain "rigid flexibility" 74

Guideline 14: Don't speak out of anger 78

Guideline 15:
    Make sure your child knows that you love her unconditionally 84

SECTION 2: THE HEALTH PUZZLE — 89

Puzzle Piece 1: Exercise 92

Puzzle Piece 2: Get enough sleep 98

Puzzle Piece 3: Eat healthy foods 102

Eat Healthy Guideline 1: Keep your child hydrated 104

Eat Healthy Guideline 2: Eat low on the food chain 107

Eat Healthy Guideline 3: Eat fresh and unprocessed foods 109

Eat Healthy Guideline 4: Eat smaller portions 111

Eat Healthy Guideline 5: Eat mindfully 112

Eat Healthy Guideline 6: Eat more often 114

Eat Healthy Guideline 7: Remember, fitness feels better 115

Eat Healthy Guideline 8: Don't overdo junk food 117

Eat Healthy Guideline 9: Eliminate something unhealthy 118

SECTION 3: FAMILY SAFETY PRINCIPLES — 121

Family Safety Principle 1: Create safe habits 124

Family Safety Principle 2: Be aware but not on guard 128

Family Safety Principle 3: Trust your intuition 132

Family Safety Principle 4: Take immediate action 136

Family Safety Principle 5:
    Learn from your and other's experience 140

Family Safety Principle 6: Communicate with confidence 144

Family Safety Principle 7:
    Follow the five steps of bully prevention 148

Family Safety Principle 8:
    Dispel the myth of not talking with strangers 152

Family Safety Principle 9: Know who to ask for help 156

Family Safety Principle 10: When in doubt, get out 160

Family Safety Principle 11: No! Go! Yell! Tell! 164

SECTION 4: WHY MARTIAL ARTS   167

SECTION 5: SCHOOL SUCCESS TIPS   173

SECTION 6: SUCCESS IN EXTRACURRICULAR ACTIVITIES   179

EPILOGUE   187

Foreword

BY: DR. ROBYN SILVERMAN

POWERFUL WORDS CHARACTER DEVELOPMENT

My father was a modern-day wise man. A veracious reader with a genius IQ, people referred to him as the "human encyclopedia" and sought his advice on everything from legal matters to financial trouble. He would listen without judgment and speak without condescending. And as much as he was in the know, he would never gossip or talk ill of others.

I was fortunate enough to know him as "Dad." When I was playing in a sports game, he made every effort to be there. When I was singing on stage, he never missed it. And when things got tense, we'd go to lunch and talk it out.

My mother and I have a wonderful, close relationship but it was my Dad, throughout my preteen and teen years, with whom I spoke most candidly. He was the one who I talked to about friendship issues. He was the one I went to when I struggled to find my footing in math. He was the one who I confided in when I was contemplating a deeper relationship with my long-time boyfriend. Yes, he was the one. Perhaps that might surprise some people but it's the truth.

You see, there is a myth that has been circulating for decades—perhaps centuries—that fathers don't matter as much as mothers. This, to put it bluntly, is just plain wrong. Every child is born with an innate, pre-programmed desire for a strong, close, reciprocal relationship with his or her father. This yearning goes both ways. As renowned pediatrician and researcher Kyle Pruett wrote, "Children and fathers hunger for each other early, often, and for a very long time." Study after study shows that those who have the privilege of such a relationship have a much better chance than those who don't to grow up feeling confident, strong and secure in a world that is sometimes difficult
to navigate.

The myth has additional facets that fathers are more important to the successful development of boys than of girls. But again, this is simply not true. In my book, GOOD GIRLS DON'T GET FAT: HOW WEIGHT OBSESSION IS MESSING UP OUR GIRLS & HOW WE CAN HELP THEM THRIVE DESPITE IT, girls detail how their confidence in themselves and what they had to offer the world wavered or stayed strong dependent on how their dads treated and responded to them. I quote Meg Meeker at the start of my father chapter, who writes in her own book, STRONG DADS, STRONG DAUGHTERS, "If you fully understand just how profoundly you can influence your daughter's life, you would be terrified, overwhelmed or both." The bullet point here: Your daughters need you just as much as your sons do.

You see, fathers do indeed provide a template for their sons of what it means to be a man. They shape their sons' identity, influence their values, and show them how to treat others and stand up for what they believe to be right. And that is monumentally important. But they also provide for their daughters an understanding, whether accurate or not, of what boys and men value in girls and women. And, beyond that, a girl's strong relationship with Dad also means lower likelihood of teen pregnancy, higher academic achievement, lower incidence of risky behavior and more positive risk-taking, just to name a few. I know. Big stuff.

No father needs to be perfect. He just needs to show up, try, adjust and try again. In one of the final days of my father's life, he told me he could have been a better dad. He thought he could have been more "there." But what he didn't realize and what I told him that day was that he was there in everything I did. He modeled for me when to speak up and when to listen; when to raise my hand in support and how to respectfully challenge the facts; when to buckle down and how to bring integrity and hard work to everything I do.

And now that he's gone, these lessons remain with me everyday. They are part of the character curriculum I write for kids, part of the presentations I give at colleges and businesses across the US and part of the interviews I do for the press across the world. I hear his voice in all the major choices I make in my life just as if he is sitting across the table from me.

We are, of course, talking about legacy. We all create it in life and leave it to others in death. It is long standing and complex but the questions for all of us are simple. If today was your last day on Earth, what legacy will you leave? What legacy do you want to leave? And perhaps most importantly, are these two things congruent?

If they are, congratulations. You are well on your way to creating strong, stable children who are likely to become confident, capable adults. And if they're not, congratulations for admitting it. Footing isn't always sure and some days are better than others. You still have time. We all have improvements to make ... both as people and as parents. Our children grow and change and, as they do, we must as well. By thinking about your legacy, your actions and your beliefs, you are being a good Dad.

A father is a teacher. He models behaviors. He councils directly. His lessons are absorbed whether intended or not. But perhaps the most evolved dads are those who are willing to learn new lessons themselves. Dave Kovar is passionate about learning new lessons. He wrote A DAD'S TOOLBOX FOR BETTER PARENTING to give dads a springboard for this learning.

When you remain open, the best lessons of how to be a powerful dad come from the very ones you aim to teach—your own children. Many of the tools in A DAD'S TOOLBOX FOR BETTER PARENTING are about paying attention to what your children are teaching you so that you, in turn, can become a better teacher to them. In fact, A DAD'S TOOLBOX FOR BETTER PARENTING urges you to team up with your children in a mutually responsive way so that both you and your children can learn from each other.

Dave Kovar's expertise as a leader and teacher in the martial arts world, as well as his own journey of fatherhood, gives him a unique perspective to speak out on what it really means to be a dad. But more than experience, Dave has a passion for helping children and their parents lead healthier, happier lives. A DAD'S TOOLBOX FOR BETTER PARENTING is a source of constant support and practical inspiration on how to be a better father ... the kind of father you want to be and your children deserve.

For more information for powerful parents:
http://www.DrRobynSilverman.com

About the author

DAVE KOVAR

A father of two, Dave Kovar is known in the martial arts world as the "Teacher's Teacher." Since 1978, Dave has inspired people not only to look and feel better but to be better. He has helped over 25,000 students of all ages develop their character and fitness through martial arts instruction through his Kovar Satori Academy of Martial Arts schools and the hundreds of martial arts schools with which he has consulted.

In addition to positively impacting his students' physical fitness, Dave has used martial arts as a vehicle to help strengthen his students' mental fitness. Over the years, he has carefully developed a system that helps his students apply the mental aspects of martial arts to excel in many areas of their lives.

The Martial Arts Industry Association (MAIA) presented Dave with its "2010 Lifetime Achievement Award" in recognition of his teaching abilities. This prestigious award has also been won by Chuck Norris and other martial arts luminaries. In 1992, the United States Martial Arts Association (USMA) honored Dave as its "Martial Arts Instructor of the Year."

Since Dave opened his first martial arts school at the age of nineteen, his reputation as an exceptionally skilled martial artist has grown. He holds the rank of black belt in ten different martial arts disciplines. In one of those disciplines, he has achieved a seventh-degree which has earned him the title of "Kyōshi."

When Dave was five years old, he saw a silhouette of a flying side kick on a billboard. He didn't even know what he was seeing, but he knew he wanted to do "that." Several years later, Dave's older brother, Tim, went away to college and took a year of tae kwon do, subsequently telling their parents that Dave should get involved in martial arts. Their first response was negative because martial arts wasn't looked upon as an appropriate hobby back in the 1970's.

After much deliberation, which included Tim pushing the matter and Dave begging, their parents acquiesced. Dave never looked back. Starting at age thirteen, he has spent every spare moment training.

Few children trained in martial arts when Dave opened his first school in 1978. Dave had a knack for it, though, and his program for children grew. Within a few years, people from all over Sacramento County were bringing their children to Dave for martial arts instruction. Eventually, his big brother

Tim became his business partner. While Tim focused on the business side, Dave was free to work on honing his teaching skills.

As their children's program grew, other martial arts school owners wanted to know what they were doing to attract students. Eventually, Tim and Dave created a video series entitled, "How to teach martial arts to kids." The first program of its kind, it was wildly successful.

They followed up with an instructor's training program called "Martial Arts Career Training." Since then, Dave Kovar's teaching methodology has influenced the entire industry. It has been a major contributor to making martial arts instruction for children a mainstream, socially accepted activity.

The brothers' next project, "Successful Life Skills for Children," was a series of huddle discussions that teach character, stranger awareness and how to deal with bullies. "Successful Life Skills for Children" is used in thousands of schools across the country.

The brothers worked together for more than twenty years. Eventually, Tim retired from the business. Dave will be forever grateful for Tim's extraordinary dedication and partnership, which began the moment Tim insightfully insisted that Dave engage in martial arts.

Dave Kovar continues to break new ground with innovations in the martial arts industry, including fitness, nutrition and character development. Revered for being a successful businessman, Dave is also a highly respected authority in optimizing personal fulfillment and in peak performance.

Dave's parenting philosophy was forged during his childhood by parents whom Dave describes as "sweet, kind and firm." His father, Leonard, is a psychologist and minister who had been a P.O.W. during World War II. Dave's mother, Lorraine, worked as an educator who was later in charge of the Head Start Program for a large public school system in Northern California.

Having survived unspeakable torment as a prisoner of war, Dave's father grew from that experience to become successful and highly sought after in his field. This meant that Dave, along with his siblings, Cindy and Tim, moved several times with their parents to such culturally diverse cities such as Boston and Bozeman, Montana, before settling in Sacramento prior to Dave's teen years.

The experience of moving frequently made Dave acutely aware of the difficulties a child faces, including bullying, when he or she is the new kid in school. In A DAD'S TOOLBOX FOR BETTER PARENTING, Dave articulates effective strategies for parents to use to address bullying, which continues to escalate in our society. It is estimated that 77% of children are bullied in some way at school in the United States.

Taught by his parents to have respect for health and fitness at an early age, Dave has spent his adult life perfecting his approach to better physical, mental and emotional fitness.

In A DAD'S TOOLBOX FOR BETTER PARENTING, Dave has incorporated the attributes of black belt excellence into a set of practical tools to help parents understand their children better so that their kids can reach their full potential.

Introduction

Whether you are a new dad or a child psychologist with ten children of your own, A DAD'S TOOLBOX FOR BETTER PARENTING was written for you.

I'm proud to say that as a professional martial arts instructor, I have taught or supervised the instruction of nearly twenty thousand children over the course of more than thirty years. A lot of the tools in A DAD'S TOOLBOX come right off the mat.

Through my interaction with students and their parents over the years I've had the privilege of seeing great parenting in action. Before having children of my own, I interviewed dozens of parents whom I felt were doing a great job in order to learn strategies that I could put to use.

In this quest to enhance my teaching skills, I have read literally hundreds of books on teaching, coaching and parenting. I came across a broad spectrum of parenting strategies, some of which were diametrically opposed to one another. However, certain concepts were consistent throughout during my research.

A DAD'S TOOLBOX FOR BETTER PARENTING weaves these common threads—what I have learned about teaching, coaching and parenting from my own experiences—into a logical, concise and easy-to-read guide to being a great dad. These principles can, of course, be applied to motherhood but I would never set myself up as an authority. I'm a dad, not a mom, and though differences may be subtle, they're there.

I've been applying these principles both to my fathering and martial arts instruction for decades and they're as useful now as they ever were.

I hope you have a great time teaming up with your son or daughter to use the tools in A DAD'S TOOLBOX FOR BETTER PARENTING.

And please note that I refer to your child as either "he" or "she" throughout the book to simplify the message, but all the tools apply to both sons and daughters.

Happy parenting!

Dave Kovar

SECTION 1
Parenting Basics
"Who is a brave person?"

The most important role you will ever have is that of "Dad." Parenting can be extremely rewarding, but it's extremely challenging, too. Just when you think you have it figured out, something happens and it's back to the drawing board.

Ben Zoma, an early spiritual sage, often asked his students, "Who is a brave person?" Zoma described "a brave person" as "someone who is smart enough to be afraid, but does whatever needs to be done anyway."

To me, "being afraid" means that certain things are to be taken seriously. Fatherhood is a real responsibility. Like it or not, we're responsible for helping to shape our child's life. We should not take this lightly.

> ***Sow a thought, reap an action.***
>
> ***Sow an action, reap a habit.***
>
> ***Sow a habit, reap a character.***
>
> ***Sow a character, reap a destiny.***

The above quote, attributed to Ralph Waldo Emerson, is one of my favorites. First and foremost, a father's job is to do his best to raise his child to become a confident, healthy, happy and contributing member of society. In order to do this, dads need to help their children think in proactive, positive ways and develop strong self-images that will guide them through rough times.

The following *Parenting Guidelines* are designed to support your success as a father. You have probably heard every one of these guidelines before. Most of them are common sense. However, knowing *what* to do and understanding *how* to do it are often two separate challenges. A DAD'S TOOLBOX FOR BETTER PARENTING unites the *what* with the *how* for a logical, easy-to-use guide to fatherhood.

As you read, you might think that I'm exaggerating the importance of being positive with your child. Guilty as charged! In my experience of working with thousands of parents over the course of more than thirty years, rarely have I come across parents who are too positive with their children. I have, however, frequently seen parents spend way too much time criticizing and being negative with their children. At the other end of this spectrum, though more rare, are parents who believe their children can do no wrong. Both approaches are off kilter.

That is why this first section, *Parenting Guidelines*, is so crucial. It teaches positive, logical and effective parenting and communication skills in an intuitive format so that you will be able to begin to apply them immediately.

We're all busy. Even with the best of intentions, days or weeks might slip by in which we haven't used any of our parenting tools. If these tools make sense to you, you might try calendaring them into your phone or computer, even setting the alarm clock on your phone as a reminder or writing yourself notes to keep in strategic locations.

GUIDELINE 1

Praise in public, but reprimand in private

There is no better feeling than receiving public recognition from someone we respect. We should be constantly looking for opportunities to praise our children openly.

Praise

Appreciation

Celebration

Encouragement

Respect

Dignity

DESCRIPTION

Don't miss any opportunity to let your child know he did a great job. Rewarding him in the moment is the way to encourage his great attitude and excellent effort.

Most of us have experienced public humiliation sometime in our life. For many people, these memories haunt them forever. Being a parent is not easy. Sometimes we get angry and want to "teach our child a lesson." But it's important to remember that no matter how angry we are or what our child has done, we should not humiliate or reprimand him in front of others. The best way is to cool down first and then address the matter privately.

A GREAT EXAMPLE

Sensei Bruce was my first karate teacher. He is a good guy and I'm happy to say that, forty years later, we're still in touch. Back in those days, not a lot of children took martial arts and there was no thought put into teaching methodology. Public praise and positive reinforcement were not in Sensei Bruce's arsenal. As a matter fact, I don't think I ever heard him say anything positive about me during those first couple of years training. It wasn't that he was rude or mean, he just didn't think to give any of his students any positive feedback.

One day, my father came into the school to pick me up. He was a bit early, so he sat down for a few moments to watch the remaining part of class. Unbeknownst to me, Sensei Bruce had decided to promote me to blue belt at the close of class. In front of the class and my father, he said aloud, "Dave, he's a tiger. He is doing great and could be a champion someday. Tonight I'm awarding him his blue belt. He certainly deserves it." I can't tell you how amazing it made me feel to have my instructor tell my dad and the rest of class that I was doing so well. I was on cloud nine the whole way home. I've never forgotten that incident. It reminds me to pass on public praise to my children and my students whenever possible.

ROOM FOR IMPROVEMENT

When I was young, I was at a party at my friend's house where there were dozens of guests of all ages. After dinner, all the kids were told to rinse their plates off and put them in the dishwasher. My friend forgot to do this and left his dish on the counter. Seeing this, his father jumped at the chance to "teach him a lesson." In front of everyone, he berated his son. I'll never forget my friend's pain and embarrassment at being publicly humiliated.

TOOL 1: Like Indiana Jones, go on a treasure hunt. Instead of looking for an ark, search for opportunities to praise your child during your normal, daily activities. These moments could occur at the grocery store, social gatherings, talking with friends on the phone or just about anywhere where you and your child are with other people. It might take practice but praising your child in public will soon come naturally.

GUIDELINE 2

Believe in your child's potential

Probably the single most important factor that will increase your child's overall success in life is your own belief that she can succeed.

Belief

Expectancy

Vision

Conviction

DESCRIPTION

Your belief in your child's potential is very powerful. As parents, we need to know and believe that our children have the ability to succeed. Then we must act accordingly. Amazing things will happen.

A GREAT EXAMPLE

I remember TJ as we'd met yesterday. This young boy was from India. TJ was very bright, but terribly shy and quite possibly the most uncoordinated child that I had ever taught. After his first introductory lesson, his father asked me point blank, "What do you think? Can he ever be any good at this? Do you think he can ever be a Black Belt?" Not wanting to disappoint the father or lower TJ's self esteem more than it already was, I lied. I told them that, although it would be difficult, I had complete faith in TJ and I knew that, if he stuck it out, he would one day earn his Black Belt. The father responded by saying, "Well, you're the expert. If you believe that he can do it, that is good enough for me. Let's get him signed up."

The guilt started the moment they left and continued to build to the point that I was sick to my stomach. I had completely sold out. There was NO way in this lifetime that TJ would ever even earn his yellow belt, let alone his Black Belt. How could I mislead this nice family? Tim, my brother and business partner, was able to calm me down a bit by reminding me that TJ had nowhere to go but up and that our program would help even him.

I decided to make helping TJ succeed my personal project. I made sure to give him a lot of attention and encouragement. Over time, a funny thing began to happen ... TJ started to get it and before long, he successfully passed his yellow belt test.

Five years later, I found him in front of me, amongst a group of newly promoted Junior Black Belts. He had done it and quite well at that! After the test, he and his dad asked to speak privately with me. The father began to express his appreciation for the program and how much it had done for TJ. Then TJ said, "Thanks for believing in me. I never thought I could do it, but you were so sure that I could and I didn't want to let you down."

TJ continued to train for a few more years. He grew into a fine young man. The last time we talked, he was in medical school. I've lost touch with him now, but I hope our paths will cross again because I never really got the chance to thank him. Looking back, I realize that I learned way more from TJ than he ever learned from me. He taught me how to be a better teacher. He showed me what perseverance really is. Most importantly, he demonstrated the power of believing in someone.

ROOM FOR IMPROVEMENT

Early on in my career, I attended a Zig Zigler seminar. At this seminar, I heard him share a statistic about inmates in the Texas State Penitentiary. He said that over fifty-percent of the inmates were told by their parents when they were young that they would end up in prison.

While an interesting statistic, I didn't fully believe it until I saw firsthand this exact thing happen. Daniel was ten years old when he and his sister enrolled in our martial arts school. Both were good children, but it was clear that they had a hard life. Their grandmother was raising them. Over time, I found out that their dad was an alcoholic and a drug addict with whom they barely had contact. Their mother was incarcerated and wouldn't be eligible for parole for several years.

I saw their dad only one time. He came into the school to watch them compete in a small tournament. It was obvious that Daniel wanted to do well for his father. When he won his match, I heard his dad say, "It is going to take a lot more than that to impress me, Danny. You'll probably wind up just like your mother." I've never been so close to kicking someone in my life! (Okay, I've kicked lots of people. I'm a martial artist. But only in training, never in anger.)

Daniel and Sarah trained with me for years after that incident. Eventually, they drifted away from the school. Later, I learned from Sarah that Daniel was doing time for car theft.

I know that Daniel and Sarah's parents were extreme, but, there's a lesson to be learned from them. Every now and then, I drive by the house Daniel and Sarah lived in when I knew them. After my thoughts wander to Daniel and where he might be now, they return to my children in the present. You can be sure that the next conversation I have with my children will be one in which I affirm their potential.

TOOL 2: Every morning as you are brushing your teeth, ask yourself if your words and actions have been congruent with your belief in your child's potential. If not, decide how you will affirm your child's potential that day.

GUIDELINE 3

Walk your talk

Children pay attention to everything we do as parents. What we do has a far greater impact on our children than what we say.

Leadership

Integrity

Honesty

Example

Consistency

DESCRIPTION

We set the best example for our children when we live and act honestly and in keeping with our own integrity without compromise. We keep our eye on the big picture—our own integrity and the character development of our children—rather than compromise our integrity and honesty for short-term gain.

A GREAT EXAMPLE

I remember being in line with my father to buy tickets for a movie one time when I was a kid. I was fourteen years old, but I looked about eleven. I mentioned to my father that if he said I was twelve, we could save a couple of bucks off the price of admission. (I had a friend whose father did that all the time and it seemed like a logical thing to do.) I will never forget what happened next. He looked at me and said, "My honesty is worth a whole lot more than the two dollars I'll save from lying about your age." I still hear those words repeated in my head every time I think about cutting a corner.

ROOM FOR IMPROVEMENT

I am always learning how to be a better parent. However much I try to be a good example for my children, I still end up being a hypocrite sometimes. A great example of this was when my son was taking Driver's Ed. I hadn't realized how many basic driving rules that I was breaking until he reminded me. It's lucky he wasn't a highway patrolman because I would have lost my license for sure.

At first, I used the excuse that I had been driving for thirty-five years and I know what I'm doing. Not only did he not buy it but I felt totally hypocritical saying it. So I decided that the best thing that I could do for my son was to do a better job in following the rules of the road.

TOOL 3: List three ways that you can be a better example to your child. Then follow through and implement them.

A Dad's Toolbox for Better Parenting

GUIDELINE 4

Constantly catch your child "doing things right"

When you are in the habit of catching your child doing things right you reinforce appropriate behavior. Everything goes better.

Alertness

Observation

Appreciation

Reinforcement

DESCRIPTION

Most of us don't need to be reminded to correct our children when they are messing up because we do that enough already. However, we do need to look out for what our children do right and, when we see something, make sure to tell them about it.

Unfortunately, following kids around and showing them everything they don't do so well is quite common with parents. Upper and lower income, functional and dysfunctional families ... it doesn't seem to matter. "Let me show you another thing that you did wrong" seems to be a common parenting technique.

A GREAT EXAMPLE

I have a friend of mine who utilizes praise as a parenting strategy unwaveringly. Everyday, he looks for something that each of his children did right—a neat, well-done homework assignment, putting the dirty clothes in the hamper or loading the dishwasher after dinner. Whatever it is, he makes a point to "catch them doing things right."

Of course, he still corrects his children and makes suggestions when needed but those corrections and suggestions are easier for his children to swallow because of all the good stuff he's catching them doing.

ROOM FOR IMPROVEMENT

As a child, I spent a lot of time down the street at the Gray's house. They had a pool, a billiards table and a whole lot of ice cream in the freezer. The only drawback was Mrs. Gray. All the kids referred to her as the "neighborhood nag." She was constantly on both of her boys and, for that matter, her boys' friends. Nothing was ever done well enough to suit her. She constantly found fault.

One day, Mr. Gray asked his sons and me to clean up the kitchen before Mrs. Gray got home. We went to it, almost excited as we anticipated Mrs. Gray's compliment on a job well done. Upon her return, the boys raced out to meet her excited to show her what we had accomplished.

Instead of appreciating our efforts, she complained that the floor hadn't been swept and the garbage had not been emptied. I remained friends with the Gray boys for years to come. I didn't see them try to please their mother after that incident. After all, pleasing her was impossible. Why even try?

Over the years, their relationship with their mother continued to deteriorate until, last I heard, they no longer had contact with her. I know she loved her boys but in her attempt to "make them better" she never praised their efforts or caught them doing things right.

Mrs. Gray taught me a lot of what not to do as a parent. Correcting my children is necessary at times but I spend more time looking for what they're doing right. The more I look, the more I discover.

TOOL 4: Every day, make it a point to catch your child doing at least three things right.

GUIDELINE 5

Set boundaries and stick to them

Children like to know where the boundaries are even when they complain about them. Boundaries make them feel safe.

Clarity

Consistency

Firmness

Fairness

Consequences

Safety

DESCRIPTION

Your child is going to test the boundaries. That's his job but if you set realistic boundaries and stick to them, things usually work out pretty well.

Don't be too quick to set boundaries to which you will not or cannot adhere. Suggestions and encouragement are a great source of motivation. However, when they don't work and it's necessary to set clear boundaries, do so and don't deviate from the boundaries you set.

A GREAT EXAMPLE

We used to take a lot of road trips as a family when I was a kid. All five of us would hop into the family compact car and head off for a family vacation, which was usually at least six states away. These trips always started out fine. We were a little cramped in the car but had fun just the same. Most evenings we would camp out. Rarely would it be in an official campsite. Usually it was on a frontage road just off the highway. My dad's philosophy was to make good time, drive until you're dead tired and then pull over anywhere, throw the sleeping bags down and call it a night.

Usually, we'd get to stay one night in a motel as a special treat. This was a big deal for us. Generally it was the middle of summer. We had no air conditioning. There were five of us stuffed into a four-seater. We were all excited by the thought of swimming in the motel pool and enjoying the luxury of beds, my dad included.

On one trip, we were driving from California to Minnesota to see relatives. On the third day of the trip, my dad announced that it would be "motel night" that night. By this time, we three children were restless and pretty tired of each other. The teasing started and went on for hours. My mom and dad asked us to quit fighting several times but we had had it and weren't listening. Finally, my dad had had enough and laid down some strong boundaries. He told us that we would drive straight through to Minneapolis instead of stopping at a motel if we didn't shape up. We calmed down for a few moments but I don't think any of us really believed him. He gave us one last warning but we still didn't listen.

True to his word, my dad drove all night and halfway into the next day until we arrived in Minneapolis. It was a rough night and one I didn't forget. Needless to say, we got the point. On our return trip to California, we shaped up when he asked us to because we knew he'd stick to his boundaries. And yes, that motel pool in Wells, Nevada was the best swim ever!

ROOM FOR IMPROVEMENT

Several years ago, my wife and I had were dining in a nice restaurant when I was startled by a rather loud, authoritative voice behind me saying, "If you don't eat all your peas, you can't have any dessert."

I glanced over my shoulder to see a young couple and their 5-year old daughter. The father's statement had caught my attention and I was curious as to how events would unfold. The couple's daughter obviously didn't like peas and she let her parents know that.

Pretty soon I heard, "Eat half of your peas and you can have dessert," followed minutes later by, "You need to eat at least one spoonful of peas if you want dessert." Shortly there after, I saw the waiter replace a plate full of peas with a big bowl of ice cream.

I'm not sure how many peas the little girl ate but my guess is not many. This young couple loved their daughter. They were trying their best to be good parents. The problem was that, if they continued to set boundaries with their daughter but failed to keep them, they would eventually become powerless as parents.

I was especially intrigued by this event because my daughter was the same age at the time. It made me wonder if my wife and I ever did the same thing with our children and that, perhaps, we were just not aware of it. The two of us talked it over and decided that, although we were probably not nearly as bad as the couple we had witnessed at dinner, we could do better.

We decided that, when boundaries did need to be set, we'd do so and that not even an act of Congress would be able to get us to move them.

> *TOOL 5: Decide if the boundaries you have currently set for your child are realistic. If they aren't, adjust them. Make sure that everyone in the house knows what the rules are and what the consequences are for breaking them. Be firm but fair.*

GUIDELINE 6
Listen

Listening is the key to all great relationships. One of the best ways to build a healthy relationship with your child is to listen to him. By listening, you show your child you care and respect him. By listening, you show your child the meaning of the words, "I love you."

Openness

Curiosity

Interest

Attention

Calm

Respect

Non-reaction

DESCRIPTION

Listening to your children seems pretty obvious. "Hearing" and "listening" are quite different, though. We often "hear" the words coming out of our children's mouths but how often do we really "listen" to what our children are saying?

Listening means that you are interested in what's going on in your child's life. Constantly remind your child that you are there for him and that he can talk to you about anything. Tell your child that, although you might not always like what he has to say, you are always there for him.

A GREAT EXAMPLE

Dana and her husband Scott are close family friends. Dana has a quality that I rarely see. She is the most amazing listener. It doesn't matter what the topic of conversation is. She takes a genuine interest in other people and their lives. People feel smart, funny and appreciated around Dana and want to share their lives with her. She listens without judgment. Good or bad, it doesn't matter. She listens. Our children have noticed it, too. She's a great example of what I constantly strive to do better with my children ... to really listen.

ROOM FOR IMPROVEMENT

My daughter and I were going for a walk. She was telling me about her school day in detail, but my mind was somewhere else. Finally, in the middle of a sentence she stepped in front of me, looked me in the eye and said, "Dad, be in the moment. You aren't even listening to me." Of course she was absolutely right and it wasn't the first time that she caught me being mentally checked out. I apologized and brought my attention back to the present moment. We had a great conversation and I really appreciated being able to share that moment with her.

> *TOOL 6: Take at least a few minutes everyday to listen to your child with complete focus and without judgment, comment or correction. Sometimes "conversation" doesn't include much talking. Basically just relax and listen.*

A Dad's Toolbox for Better Parenting

GUIDELINE 7

Hold your children to a high standard

It's amazing what children can accomplish when they set their minds to it and are encouraged to do their best by people they respect. "Whether the task be big or small, do it right or not at all." I remember learning this phrase from my grandmother years ago.

Expectations

Diligence

Discipline

Integrity

Effort

Fairness

Accountability

DESCRIPTION

Holding your child to a high standard can be taken to extremes. As parents, we can certainly go too far and demand either too much or too little from our children. So how do you know for sure how hard to push your child or how much to expect from her? Parenting is more of an art than a science, so we'll never know for sure. The most important thing to do is to evaluate each situation individually.

A GREAT EXAMPLE

I remember a moment one summer when my grandmother called me to task after inspecting the mediocre job I had done mowing their backyard. She very nicely told me that I was capable of doing much better. She explained to me that my grandfather would be home within an hour and that there was plenty of time left to get the job done right. Begrudgingly, I stepped up my game. You know what? It felt pretty good when my grandfather raved about how the lawn had never looked better and what a great job I had done. My grandmother winked at me. We shared a secret that afternoon and, to this day, I'm better for it.

ROOM FOR IMPROVEMENT

Early on in my career, I had a young student named Johnny. Just after Johnny enrolled, his mom pulled me aside to let me know that Johnny had some learning disabilities and couldn't be expected to progress at the same rate as other kids. She asked me if I would be patient with him and not push him too hard.

Of course, I agreed and Johnny's training began. It was a good thing that I didn't push him too hard because he was progressing slower than other children ... or so I thought. A few months into his training I took a week's vacation and had one of my senior students teach Johnny's class for me. Tom was eager and had a good knack for working with young children, but he was inexperienced.

In my excitement to leave for vacation I forgot to tell Tom that he should take it easy on Johnny. I thought nothing of this until my flight home. My heart began to race as I envisioned getting a lecture from Johnny's mom about her son being pushed too hard. Even worse yet, I imagined Johnny experiencing humiliation because he could not keep up with the rest of the class while I was gone.

Much to my surprise, I returned to find Johnny performing at a much higher level than I had thought possible. He was proud of his new skills and so was his mother. What had changed while I had been gone? Tom had no preconceived ideas of Johnny's limitations. Therefore, he held him to a higher standard and Johnny happily rose to the occasion.

> *TOOL 7: Ask yourself these questions—Is it realistic for me to expect more of my child here? If so, how much? For this situation, what is the best way to encourage my child to do better?*

GUIDELINE 8

Inspire your child to greatness

In most cases, parents are the most influential people in a child's life. Therefore, it is very important that you try to make your interactions with your child as positive and uplifting as possible.

Opportunity

Positivity

Communication

Confidence

Expectation

Completion

Success

DESCRIPTION

Every day is filled with opportunities to plant positive seeds in your child's mind. Children (especially young children) are blank canvases waiting to be painted. You can give your child a new way to think about how he views himself. And you can literally put new words in your child's head for him to use later.

Rather than being disappointed in or critical of your child, you can turn the situation into a challenge for him to perform at a higher level. Even though he might feel as if he is facing an insurmountable difficulty, show him that he can overcome obstacles and still function. With repetition, your child will begin to know that he can do what is required, even when it isn't easy. For example, your child might think, "I don't feel like doing my homework today, but my dad expects me to do it because he knows that I can do it even when I'm tired."

So, instead of falling prey to sympathizing or agreeing with your child's diminished view of himself, be sure to build up your child's confidence and inspire him to greatness.

A GREAT EXAMPLE

A friend of mine has four children, all of them bright, grounded and happy. I asked him what his basic viewpoints on parenting were and I was not a bit surprised to hear his answer.

He said, "I constantly remind them how smart and capable they are and how proud I am of all the hard work and effort they put into all of their activities. And I make sure to tell them this even before they start a new project."

ROOM FOR IMPROVEMENT

As a child, I played baseball for a few seasons. Coach Coursey was my friend's dad and a good guy with the best of intentions. During the summer of my last season, I was at the Coursey's house playing with my friend. The coach came out and we had a nice talk about baseball, our last season and the future. Then he definitively told me that I wasn't very good at team sports, but was better at individual sports.

At the time, I accepted Coach Coursey's comment as fact. I excelled at sports I perceived to be "individual" sports. Because I respected Coach Coursey, I believed what he said to be true. After that season, I didn't pursue team sports. Instead, I excelled at wrestling, skiing and karate. (Later I realized that martial arts, a sport I perceived to be an individual sport, is very much a team sport.) The coach was unaware of the impact of his words on me.

As an adult, I've learned that I am a pretty good team player after all. However, Coach Coursey's one statement that summer afternoon years ago had a profound effect on my belief system which took me literally decades to undo.

> *TOOL 8: Remind your child of how capable he is at least twice everyday. Constantly affirm him, believe in him and let him feel his own potential. Be delighted that he's dreaming big. And never make him feel foolish for having such big dreams.*

GUIDELINE 9

Choose your battles wisely

Sometimes you just have to let your child be. Sometimes you just have to look the other direction. Of course, with issues of safety or morality you should address the issue promptly. But when you're dealing with less important issues, remember always to choose your battles wisely.

Flexibility

Openness

Prioritizing

Humanity

Compassion

Ease

DESCRIPTION

Pope John Paul II was once asked what the best way was to get along with others. He replied, "See everything, overlook a lot, and correct a little." This is great advice! It's applicable to every type of relationship but especially to the parent-child relationship.

We probably all know someone who endlessly nitpicks at his child. That someone might even be us. We all want to help our children be all that they can be. Constantly correcting them might seem logical but this strategy almost always has the reverse effect on children.

Excessive exposure to negative comments only strengthens your child's need to protect himself and defy you. To be excessively concerned with or critical of inconsequential details creates distance between you and your child. Nobody's perfect and your child is no exception. Why, then, nitpick?

If you are on him about everything, pretty soon he won't listen to you regarding anything. The day you are able to resist commenting on his mismatched wardrobe or shaggy haircut, the fact that he left his socks in the living room, his talking with his mouth full or that the slang he uses isn't proper English, is probably the day that he will be more receptive to whatever important input you do give him.

A GREAT EXAMPLE

Growing up, my father was relatively lenient compared to some of my friends' dads. Maybe he could afford to be lenient because my brother, sister and I weren't real big troublemakers. Sure, we got into trouble from time to time and we didn't always get along but overall our parents didn't need to resort to strict discipline. I felt my parents were pretty reasonable people. I was given plenty of freedom as long as my attitude was right and my grades stayed decent.

My father had a motorcycle when he was growing up. He used to tell us about his experiences riding (mostly in disbelief that his dad let him have a bike in the first place because of all the dumb things that he did). He told my brother and me more than once that he didn't feel motorcycles should be in our future.

I wanted one, however. So when I had a chance to buy a motorcycle from a friend at a bargain price at age seventeen, I jumped at the chance. As I was driving it home for the first time, I imagined the conversation that my father and I would have. I wasn't too concerned. I knew that, eventually, I would be able to talk him into letting me keep it.

Upon first glance, my father looked at me and, in a stern voice, he said, "Nice bike. Sell it." Then he reached out and took the keys from me. My first ride on that motorcycle was also my last. I didn't question his decision. I didn't try to change his mind. I knew in that one instant that motorcycle riding was nonnegotiable.

ROOM FOR IMPROVEMENT

When my son was in grade school, I volunteered when I could and went on virtually every field trip from kindergarten to sixth grade. Over the years, I got to know the kids and their parents pretty well.

There is always a troublemaker or two in every school and my son's school was no different. Seth was one of these. A difficult child to like, Seth was constantly doing the wrong things for the wrong reasons.

Dealing with Seth's dad wasn't much easier. Seth's dad was ruthless in his parenting. He constantly argued and found fault with Seth, even when he didn't deserve it. One particular incident stands out in my mind.

I was carpooling for a day trip to a museum in Berkeley and Seth was in my car. We got along pretty well and he wasn't much trouble that day. When I dropped him off back at school, his dad was waiting for him. He walked up to the car and said, "Okay, what did Seth do today that I should know about?"

I responded by telling his father that Seth had a good day and I had nothing negative to report. At that moment, his father looked over at Seth (who had been eating Cheetos the whole way home and was covered with orange Cheetos goo) and chewed him out for being dirty. I can't help but think that Seth's challenges were due, at least in part, to his father's abrasiveness, relentlessness and inability to choose his battles wisely.

> *TOOL 9: Make a list of all the things that you currently nitpick your child about. Decide which of these things you are willing to tolerate for now and then commit yourself to the concept of looking the other way when you see them happening. Finally, for every one thing that you decide to correct your child on, make it a habit to find at least one other thing (and, preferably, two) to praise him for.*

GUIDELINE 10

Be easily in awe

Make the decision to allow yourself to be impressed often by your child.

Joy

Amazement

Receptivity

Delight

DESCRIPTION

Being easily in awe is really about appreciating the time and effort your child puts into a project. And it's about letting her know how great she did. Your child needs your approval and wants you to be impressed when she has done something well.

I am not talking about "false praise," which can have a detrimental effect. False praise comes in many forms and usually we give it when we are not paying attention. For example, when your daughter shows you the finger painting she did in kindergarten, false praise might sound like a quick, "That's nice," as you carry on with your business.

Instead take a minute to pay attention and admire her artwork. Sincere praise resonates and might sound like, "Wow, I love it! There's a lot of blue here. You must really like blue. I really like how you mixed the blue with red to make purple. Can I put this on the refrigerator so everyone can see my-daughter-the-artist's latest project? Keep up the great work. I'm proud of you."

Although you might quickly forget the interaction, your child will not. Your kind words will be ingrained on her psyche for years and will probably become part of her belief system for the rest of her life.

A GREAT EXAMPLE

When I was in sixth grade, my teacher, Mrs. Austin, had the students write a book report and give an oral presentation on that same book. I don't remember what book I chose, but I do remember the conversation I had with Mrs. Austin directly after giving my oral report. She pulled me aside and said, "Wow, Dave, that was really good! You have excellent comprehension."

I'm sure Mrs. Austin wouldn't remember this conversation, but it's embedded in my psyche forever. To this day, I pride myself on having good comprehension. I have complete confidence that I will understand whatever I read very well. Why? Because Mrs. Austin told me that I have good comprehension, that's why.

ROOM FOR IMPROVEMENT

When my son, Alex, was little, I came home from work in a big hurry because I wanted to go for a run before it got dark. My son was excited to show me his drawing of a dinosaur. I quickly walked over to the kitchen table and said blandly, "That's nice, son." Then I hurried to the bedroom to change for my run. A minute later, my wife walked into the bedroom and, by the look on her face, I knew I was in trouble. She told me that Alex had spent all afternoon drawing the dinosaur picture just for me and that he had asked her several times if he thought I would like it. My response wasn't what he had expected. He was disappointed that he wasn't the artist he thought he was. I mean after all, his dad hardly looked at it.

Of course, I went back out into the kitchen and reexamined Alex's drawing in detail. I would be a bit late for my run, but that was a small price to pay. I really paid attention and sincerely told him how wonderful it was. Although my belated response certainly helped, it would have helped a lot more if I had been in awe of him the first time. How much more time would that have taken? Thirty seconds! I vowed to do a better job of being easily in awe after that experience.

TOOL 10: Be impressed by your child at least once everyday and then let her know.

GUIDELINE 11

Give your child choices, not ultimatums

Give your child choices rather than ultimatums to empower him to take action to resolve the problem.

Choices

Logic

Calm

Control

Breath

Clarity

Empowerment

DESCRIPTION

A very common parental response to a misbehaving child is "the ultimatum." For example, "If you don't stop bothering your sister we are leaving Disneyland immediately and driving straight home." Giving this ultimatum can feel momentarily satisfying but you'll usually regret it soon afterwards because you know that you won't follow through. And therein lies the problem. Your child knows that, too.

You may think that giving an ultimatum keeps you in control of your child but the reverse is true. And every time you don't follow up on an ultimatum, you lose credibility with him.

Logic and emotion are like oil and water. They don't mix. When we become emotional, we don't think clearly. We are likely to say and do things that we really don't mean. The next time you find yourself about to issue your child an ultimatum, stop and take a few deep breaths instead.

When your child is acting out, take a moment to breathe deeply and calm down. You'll be more likely to see the issue for what it is and respond more logically in a way that better fits the situation. You will be able to give your child appropriate choices to empower him to take action to resolve the situation.

Then you can give your child options. For example, "Would you like to do your homework now or in 15 minutes?" Or "Do you want broccoli or spinach with your sandwich?" Likewise, "Do you want to come home at 7 o'clock or 7:30 p.m.?"

This makes your child feel more in control. When you give him a choice, you are more likely to get his cooperation.

A GREAT EXAMPLE

The Connors' children and ours grew up together. Our families were good friends and did a lot together. The Connors' youngest boy, Nicholas, came into this world testing their patience. Their older two children were incredibly well-behaved and easy, so this third child really threw them for a loop. Nicholas constantly pushed limits.

One night over dinner, young Nicholas threw peas at his big brother. This wasn't the first incident of the evening for him and I could tell that his dad was losing patience. Instead of saying, "If you don't stop that immediately, I will lock you in the closet for a week," like I sensed he wanted to, his father took a deep breath and said calmly, "Nicholas, if you stop now you can still have dessert and watch the movie with the other kids after dinner. If you don't stop immediately, you'll be done for the night and you'll get neither. It's your choice."

Because his father had followed through in the past, Nicholas knew that the consequences were real and that he had a decision to make. Nicholas made a good choice and behaved for the rest of the evening. I know it doesn't always happen like that, but it only took this one incident for me to see the value of giving choices and not ultimatums.

ROOM FOR IMPROVEMENT

The checkout line at the grocery store was long. There had to have been at least four people in front of me, all with extremely full carts. The man in front of me had two small children and was doing his best control them, but with very little success. I quickly got the impression that he was at a loss as to how to handle his kids.

Soon the ultimatums began. The first one was, "If you two don't calm down immediately, you are going to be in so much trouble when we get home." That one worked for all of ten seconds.

Next the father pulled the box of Popsicles from the cart and threatened to put them back. His two children stared at him blankly for a moment and then resumed their arguing. (By the way, the Popsicles stayed in the cart even after the ultimatum.) When that didn't work the dad lost it and yelled, "That's it! You're grounded for a month, both of you!"

I could tell that his words were empty and that he probably would not follow through. And guess what? I'm pretty sure his children knew he wouldn't, as well. Of course, that father loved his children and was doing his best to control them. Unfortunately, no one ever explained to him the importance of giving choices with logical consequences instead of ultimatums.

> *TOOL 11: Think of an ongoing challenge that you're currently facing with your child. Decide on some options that you can present to him which will give him some say in how he is going to resolve the problem.*

GUIDELINE 12

Never compare

We are all running our own race. Everyone has his own strengths and weaknesses, which is why comparing our child to other children is unfair.

Praise

Appreciation

Individuality

Celebration

Encouragement

DESCRIPTION

It's tough to never compare your child to a sibling or friend. At the very least, though, we need to minimize our comparisons. And it's very important not to vocalize them within hearing range of your child. You quit appreciating your child for who she is when you compare your child with another,

A GREAT EXAMPLE

I had a student who was an amazing athlete. This young lady was an Olympic caliber martial artist. For several years, she was the number one competitor in the country in her age group. She spent her teen years traveling and competing both nationally and internationally. This girl was born to win. Besides being a great athlete, she had a wonderful personality and a great attitude. Everyone liked her and wanted to be around her.

This young lady had a little sister three years her junior. I couldn't help but feel a little sorry for kid sister. She had serious shoes to fill. Amazingly, little sister seemed to show no resentment toward her older sibling. In fact, she was her sister's biggest fan. And I think I know why.

Her parents never compared her to her older sister. They never expected her to do the same things. They constantly affirmed her and recognized her unique gifts. One time, after my student had just won an event, I saw the family interacting and I went up to talk to them. I praised my student for another win and made some comment to her parents about how they should be proud of their daughter. Without missing a beat, her father said, "We are. We're proud of both our girls. They are both amazing in their own way." He did so while smiling and making eye contact with his youngest daughter.

At that moment, I understood why she didn't feel any jealousy towards her big sister. There was no need to. Her family loved and affirmed her for who she was. Karate champion or not, it didn't matter to her parents. They loved her just the same.

ROOM FOR IMPROVEMENT

A man wanted to enroll his two young boys in martial arts. I was absolutely stunned by how he introduced his boys to me.

He said, "This is Toby. He's twelve years old and a great athlete. He also is an excellent student. As a matter of fact, he's pretty good at everything he does.

And this is my youngest son, Nick. He's eight years old. He's not nearly the athlete his big brother is. I'm kind of worried about him because he's not very bright either. We're doing our best to have him try to be more like his big brother."

I looked over at little Nick as his father was describing him and he sadly nodded in agreement. I could almost hear him thinking, "It must be true, right? I mean, my dad wouldn't lie, would he?"

Never in my life had I witnessed such a blatant comparison. I knew this dad loved both his boys but he sure had a strange way of showing it. I pulled the father aside during the boys' orientation class to address the issue. I explained to him how damaging I felt the public comparison was that he had just made about his boys. Surprisingly, he was more receptive than I thought he would be. As a matter of fact, he thanked me and then enrolled both boys in our program right then. Both boys ended up training with me for years and earned their black belts.

Years later, I received a thank you letter from the father expressing how beneficial martial arts had been for both his boys. He also went on to say what a big impact our initial conversation had made on how he practices parenting. He told me that it had never felt right to compare his two boys, but that was what his father had done with him and his brother. He just thought that it was what parents did.

I doubt that anyone reading this book has compared their child to someone else as blatantly as this father did. With that said, it is probably not a bad idea to be mindfully aware of any comparisons that you do make.

> *TOOL 12: When you catch yourself comparing your child to others, stop immediately and ask yourself, "How can I help her run her own race?"*

GUIDELINE 13
Maintain "rigid flexibility"

Maintaining "rigid flexibility" means being more concerned with the spirit of the family rules versus the actual rules themselves. It means to set a high standard for your child while knowing that there are going to be exceptions to this standard. That's just life. In an attempt to parent well, we sometimes rigidly adhere to a rule when it doesn't make sense.

Rigid flexibility is like a willow tree in the wind. It's flexible enough to bend. Otherwise, it would break. When a situation arises in which it's obvious that being flexible is the wise decision for the greater good, we can bend.

Guidelines are very useful but every parent needs to "call an inaudible" from time to time. In other words, there are times when you will need to decide what to do at the last second after weighing all the possible options.

Flexibility

Balance

Responsiveness

Standards

Innovation

DESCRIPTION

Coach John Wooden, the legendary college basketball coach, had a specific way of working with his players. He believed in treating them the same by treating them differently. He didn't demand the same things from every player. He looked at them as individuals and then adjusted his expectations accordingly. This is the concept behind "rigid flexibility."

Parents often have a difficult time with *rigid flexibility* because they view it as being inconsistent. *Rigid flexibility* is really about balance. Some parents are too flexible with their children. They let them have way too much freedom and let them make way too many decisions on their own. Other parents are the exact opposite. They make all of the decisions for their children and they adhere to their parenting principles to a fault, never allowing for any flexibility.

The beauty of *rigid flexibility* is that it helps you to develop a set of clear guidelines that your child understands. Do your best to stick to them, but know that these guidelines won't always fit and will need to be bent a little as the situation requires.

A GREAT EXAMPLE

I learned to maintain *rigid flexibility* from my older brother, Tim. We do black belt testing three times a year in our martial arts schools, a process which has been developed and formalized over 30-years of trial and error. We are very strict on the test dates. For example, if you can't make the April test dates, then you simply have to reschedule for August. We do this because we found that, if we're the least bit flexible, we end up fielding all kinds of unrealistic requests for customized belt tests.

Several years back, we were approached by a family regarding their black belt tests. Being Seventh-day Adventists, they celebrated the Sabbath on Saturdays and could not, in good conscience, test that day.

I went to talk this over with Tim in order to formulate the proper response to this family. I was sure that he would help me find the words to explain to them the importance of coming on Saturday to test. Instead, Tim looked me in the eye and said, "Why don't we do a special test for them on Thursday night? We can't in good conscience expect them to do something incongruent with their beliefs, can we?" It seemed so logical once he said it, but I had been so ingrained in my belief pattern that the thought never occurred to me. We ended up having a Thursday test. The family did great and everyone left happy.

ROOM FOR IMPROVEMENT

In order for school-age students testing to be promoted from one rank to another in our martial arts schools, they have to show proof that they are doing well at home and in school. We do this by sending an "Intent to Promote" form home with them. They have to bring it back with signatures and approval from both their teacher and their parents.

From time to time, a child will return the form with a note from his teacher saying he is not doing well at school. When this happens, we work with the family to devise a plan of action. Most of the time, a note from the child's teacher saying that he is trying hard and moving in the right direction is enough for us to continue on with the belt promotion. The parents nearly always agree with us.

One of our students was struggling at school. He had been diagnosed with a learning disorder and, as a result, not only were his grades weak but he suffered from behavior issues, as well. He was pretty good for us while he was in class. His parents said that our class was the only place where he seemed to learn.

When his "Intent to Promote" form was returned to us, it was obvious that his grades weren't what they should be. I spoke with the parents about having his teacher send us a note indicating that he was improving, as that would be good enough for us. We didn't want to hold him back too long because we didn't want him to lose interest in martial arts. After all, martial arts was doing him a great deal of good and it seemed to be the only thing working for him.

The boy's dad refused to budge. He remained inflexible as he saw this as an opportunity to strong-arm his child to get better grades. He was the dad and I had to support his decision, but I was concerned about the effects. Once this child realized that his belt promotion was months away instead of just days, he completely lost interest in his martial arts training and the family drifted off. I can't help but think that if his father would've applied the concept of *rigid flexibility*, we could have been a strong ally in helping this child navigate through this rough time.

> *TOOL 13: Decide where you are on the "rigid flexibility" pendulum. If you feel you are either too lenient or too strict, make adjustments.*

GUIDELINE 14
Don't speak out of anger

We are all emotional beings and we tend to be more emotional with our children—in both good ways and bad ways—because we love and care for them so much. It is for this reason that we need to be extra mindful of our emotions when we are dealing with them.

Sometimes our fuse is pretty short when we're under a lot of pressure—going through a divorce, hitting a rough patch at work or experiencing relationship, money or health problems. Something your child did which normally would be mildly irksome might trigger a violent inner reaction during these times.

Make certain that you are not taking your anger and frustration with yourself or your situation out on your child. When you let your anger rip, it does a lot of damage ... some of which might be irreparable. This is why it's so vital to practice not speaking out of anger.

Awareness

Self-control

Calm

Mindfulness

Logic

Patience

Silence

DESCRIPTION

One heated argument or one angry sentence is oftentimes all it takes to drive a wedge between you and your child. Do your best to avoid this situation at all costs. Try not to speak out of anger. It is natural to lose your temper from time to time but beware of what you say when you lose your self-control. If you don't watch your words, chances are they will come back to bite you later.

Some circumstances might demand that you raise your voice to your child. However, there is a difference between raising your voice to your child because you need to get his attention and yelling at him because you lose your temper. If you lose your temper and end up saying things in the heat of the moment, you'll regret it.

Yes, you can apologize to your child and you should, but saying something out of anger and then apologizing for it later is like pounding a nail into a wall. The apology might remove the nail from the wall but the nail's hole remains. It is far better not to say anything in the first place for which you might have to apologize later.

The concept of self-control when we get angry is easy to talk about but extremely hard to put into practice. The first step is awareness. Notice when you are beginning to get angry. When you're aware of your anger, you will be able to objectify it. And what you can objectify, you can better control. Even though you're angry, this awareness will help you respond to the situation more logically. At the very least, this awareness might be all you need to keep your mouth shut until the wave of anger has passed.

A GREAT EXAMPLE

One of the highlights of raising my kids is going up to our family cabin. Wintertime, summertime, early spring ... it doesn't matter. We all love it there. It's especially enjoyable when we share our cabin with friends. On one particular trip, our friends came up in a new jet black SUV. Kyle, the father, had wanted this truck for years. It had all the bells and whistles and he was jazzed.

The following afternoon, our two sons were racing their bikes around the neighborhood. When the lunchtime bell rang, they sprinted towards the cabin, both vying to be the first back. Kyle's son, Jesse, misjudged his speed and had to swerve at the last minute to avoid hitting his little sister. Unfortunately, he ran smack dab into the side of his father's brand new truck. No one was hurt but the scratch was too big to be buffed out.

Jesse felt terrible. He knew how his dad felt about that truck and, in his child mind, he had ruined it forever. I'm not sure how I would've handled it with my son if he had scratched my new truck but I can only hope that I would handle it as well as Kyle did.

Kyle quickly saw it for what it was … an accident. I could tell that Kyle was angry, at first. It would have been easy for him to make Jesse feel even worse by scolding him, but he didn't. I could almost hear him thinking that his son's self-esteem was worth more than his brand new truck.

Kyle looked at Jesse and asked him if he was all right. Then he told him, "No worries, buddy. I know you didn't mean to do it. It's okay. We can get the truck fixed next week." They hugged. It took Jesse a few minutes to regain his composure. I looked on with a new appreciation for Kyle's parenting skills and his ability to respond with love rather than with anger.

ROOM FOR IMPROVEMENT

My daughter is an extremely happy young lady. She was born that way. If there's an exception, it's when she's choosing her outfit for the day every morning before school.

I'm not sure why this happens. The night before, she will have narrowed down the next day's attire to four choices. But when morning rolls around none of these outfits work for her. Sometimes this makes her grumpy.

One morning I had had enough. I had a lot to do at work that day and we were going to be late if she didn't decide on the right color socks to wear. Pretty quickly, I lost it. I don't remember exactly what I said, but it wasn't pretty.

Looking back on that moment now, it's hard to believe that I had thought that yelling at her would help. To the contrary, she was slower than ever and the following five minutes were miserable for everyone.

Things were tense during the ride to school that morning. Still angry, I vented, and said some things to my daughter that I still regret. Of course, later on that afternoon I apologized. But I could not erase my comments from her memory. This is why it's so important we don't speak out of anger. These aren't the kind of memories we want to create for our children.

TOOL 14: Focus on one thing your child does that makes you angry. Keep it simple. For example, you might get angry when he leaves his dirty clothes on the floor. Mindfully decide to talk to him in a logical fashion about this issue.

When you are able to be calm about the small things, you can deal with bigger issues. Next time you find yourself angry with your child over that bigger issue, do your best to take care of the immediate situation as needed while saying as little as possible. Once you calm down, go back and talk to him.

A Dad's Toolbox for Better Parenting

GUIDELINE 15

Make sure your child knows that you love her unconditionally

The most important thing you can do as a parent is to let your child know—by your words and your actions—that you love her unconditionally.

Affection

Engagement

Communication

Creativity

Constancy

DESCRIPTION

Loving your child unconditionally is an innate response for most parents and something most of us would never question. However, parents are often so busy with their daily demands that they forget to communicate their unconditional love to their child.

Nothing helps your child to feel more loved and appreciated than spending quality time with her. Create and seize opportunities to spend one-on-one time with your child, other than watching television. Engage with her, whichever activity you choose.

There are many ways to express your unconditional love for your child. In fact, the more you do this, the more ways you'll find to show your unconditional love.

Tell your child, "I love you," on a regular basis. For some parents, this is difficult. Do it anyway. Tell your child first thing in the morning, last thing at night, during an argument, after an argument … It doesn't matter exactly when you tell her. Just make sure you tell her.

There is so much you can do to let your child know that you love her! You can write her a note and put it in an unsuspected place—on the bathroom mirror in the morning, in her lunch bag or on her pillow. Or you can make something for your child—breakfast in bed, a handmade toy or a scrapbook of her last soccer season.

Finally, be there for your child when she needs you. We all fall down at times. You show your unconditional love when you are there to pick your child up regardless of what made her fall down.

A GREAT EXAMPLE

The Shepherd's had four boys, all bunched together in a 7-year time span. All four of these young men were "all boy." They were extremely physical, energetic and a bit mischievous. We affectionately referred to them as "the storm." They weren't bad, but they got into their fair share of trouble. Regardless of what happened, their parents were always there for them.

Being there for their sons didn't mean that they bailed them out of trouble or let them go unpunished. They practiced tough love. They made sure that their boys felt the consequences of their actions. With that said, their parents were always able to communicate to their boys that they loved them regardless of what they did. I remember one particular incident where the oldest boy was caught egging a neighbor's car. His father asked me if I would join forces with him in discussing the ramifications of his actions. He felt my influence in the matter would help to redirect his son's energy in the future. I was happy to oblige and the two of us met with his oldest son.

I'll never forget the father's opening sentence to his son. He looked him in the eye and said, "You know I love you, son. I'll always love you no matter what you do but this behavior is unacceptable." We determined the consequences for his actions on the spot. There were quite a few and, thankfully, the boy stepped up and did what he was asked to do to make the situation right.

Recently, I had a discussion with this young man about the incident. He commented that although his father was pretty strict with the boys growing up, he needed to be. He said that they always knew that they were loved and that this unconditional love helped him become the kind of person he wanted to be.

ROOM FOR IMPROVEMENT

My daughter's kindergarten class took a field trip to Angel Island near San Francisco. Near the end of the day, some of the children (and parents) were getting a bit cranky. It had been a long afternoon. Everyone was hungry and the thought of driving home in heavy traffic had brought everyone back to reality.

One girl in particular was having a bit of a meltdown. I don't remember what the tantrum was about but I certainly remember her dad's response. He looked at her and said, "If you don't stop whining, I'm going to leave you here to fend for yourself. There are plenty of other little girls who would appreciate your bedroom and your toys."

I wasn't the only parent who heard those comments. Several of us looked at each other in stunned disbelief, even though we knew that he didn't really mean what he said and that he was only trying to get his daughter's attention. She became hysterical and cried buckets. It took another mom quite awhile to calm her down.

I still get angry when I think about it. Put yourself in that little girl's shoes and imagine how it must have felt to have your father so ready to trade you in! Did she feel unconditionally loved? Not likely. We've all been angry with our children before. We might have even said some things we shouldn't have. But let's remember never to give our children a reason to think that we don't love them unconditionally.

TOOL 15: At least once a week, do something completely random to show your child that you love her unconditionally. If you need to, calendar it into your phone, write yourself a note and stick it on your dashboard, etc. to make sure you remember.

SECTION 2
The Health Puzzle
EXERCISE
GET ENOUGH REST
EAT HEALTHY FOODS

Your child's "Health Puzzle" has three different pieces. Exercise. Get enough rest. And eat healthy foods. Each of these pieces is vital. Together they make for a healthy child. If a piece is missing, then your child's health is compromised. Too much junk food, lack of exercise or staying up too late can lead to your child getting sick.

Can you do everything in your power and still have your child experience poor health? Of course. Some things are out of your control but there are plenty of things you can control. Why not stack the odds in favor of your child's health?

As parents we tend to overcomplicate things—including our children's health. In most cases, it's so much simpler than we make it. We can keep our children pretty healthy if we stick to a few basic concepts.

Sometimes it's difficult to know how to begin to build the *Health Puzzle* with our children. No worries. The *Health Puzzle* is simple, practical and fun! You can have a great time teaming up with your child to be healthy.

Here are some practical, simple ideas to complete your child's health puzzle.

HEALTH PUZZLE PIECE 1

Exercise

This section on exercise probably wouldn't have been necessary thirty years ago. Just like many of you I spent my childhood outside riding my bike, climbing trees or playing in the street. There was no need for public service announcements to tell children to exercise.

When I was a child there weren't as many overweight children. We didn't have video games, computers or cable TV. The only sedentary activity available to us was reading (and that vigorously exercised our minds).

In the last three decades, I've witnessed the deteriorating level of physical fitness in children firsthand. My research shows that children spend an average of 5-hours a day on media-driven activities. Also, that one-third of children in America are overweight or obese and that these children are much more likely to develop serious illnesses. Due to budget cuts, most schools don't offer daily physical education classes and those that do have minimal programs.

Early on in my martial arts program, I used the same warm-up in my classes for all my students regardless of level. Over the years, however, I've found it necessary to lessen the physical requirements for beginners because they're starting at a much lower level of fitness. This is due to the increasing lack of exercise in children's daily lives.

Consistency

Fun

Action

Movement

Strength

Flexibility

Endurance

Play

Run

Jump

Roll

Fall

Crawl

Explore

DESCRIPTION

Engage with your child in general physical activity. Not only is general physical activity important to keep your child at the right weight, physical activity is essential to your child's development emotionally, intellectually, socially and physically. In short, children need to keep their bodies moving. The human body thrives on movement and a child's developing body especially so. Children need to run, jump, climb, fall, crawl, roll and cartwheel to develop correctly.

Exercising can be a great opportunity to play and interact with your child. Make it fun. Everyone needs to play regardless of age. Having a child is a fabulous excuse to do just that ... to be a kid again.

Years ago, The National Geographic featured "animals at play" in one of its issues. The article explained that playing is the way that the young animals learn to survive as they grow. Young animals are often taught survival skills by their elders through play. Playing with their peers is vital to their survival because it gives them a chance to practice moving, responding and reacting to different situations. Young creatures of just about every species, including humans, need to play a lot.

Your child needs at least one hour of physical exercise each day. Do your best to incorporate activities for the entire family into your everyday. Instead of making exercise something your child *has* to do, make it something you and your child *gets* to do. And remember that your child's long-term health is in the balance. Your attitude and example will set the tone. You're wired to protect your child. What better protection can a dad provide than to make sure his child grows up healthy and strong? What can you as a father do to help your child develop a lifelong habit of exercise for a healthy future?

HEALTH PUZZLE PIECE 1 TOOL: The possibilities for incorporating exercise into your and your child's daily routines are endless. Come up with a few ideas of your own and then brainstorm with your child. Create a simple plan. The key is to keep it simple and be consistent.

TIPS:

Limit your child's access to media.
How you spend your time has a lot to do with how much you exercise. You can encourage more exercise simply by eliminating or lessening access to media at home. Make sure your plan includes the types of exercise you and your child choose to do, but also what you need *not to do* in order be more active and fit.

Past generations didn't have to deal with the media issue. In the past, children didn't have a lot of options that weren't physically demanding. There weren't video games, computers and television with a gazillion channels to distract children. To keep from being bored children were nearly always doing something physical. This is why the modern parent has to be more actively involved in their child's physical development.

Exercise with your child consistently and make it fun.
Probably the single two most important factors in developing a healthy exercise for your family are consistency and fun. If it isn't fun, your child will not want to do it. Team up with your child to design exercise or "play" time.

The sky's the limit on exercise ideas. There are the simple things like bike riding, hiking, kicking a soccer ball, playing Frisbee, etc., all of which are great options. Also, you can start a formal exercise routine with your child where you do specific exercises together. And there are fabulous exercise and sports programs and classes—especially, martial arts—out there for children and adults. (You'll learn more about the benefits of martial arts in *Section 4: Why martial arts will help you raise a healthier and happier child*.) The gift of exercise is one of the most valuable gifts you can give your child.

Power walk
Instead of driving to the park or to the store, power walk. Power walking is "to walk with attitude." Your child will respond right away if you ask him to have attitude. You can make it into a game. Time your walks. Each time, try to match or beat your last time. For example, "Alright kids, the last time we walked to the park it took twelve minutes. Let's see if we can do it today in ten."

Bike riding

If you're anything like me, you grew up on your bike. What better memories do you have than racing around the neighborhood with your friends on your two-wheeler? When your children are younger, go on frequent rides with them. It doesn't have to be an all-day expedition. Even a short ride around the neighborhood on a regular basis can do wonders for everyone in your family. As your child gets older, encourage him to turn off the TV and video games and get out on her bike. She might need a push at first but once she gets outside you probably won't see her for a while. Children need to be reminded. Changing habits takes practice. And it's easy to forget how much more fun bike riding is than watching television (at least until going outside becomes second nature).

Swimming

Swimming is a great activity. Nearly every child loves to swim. The challenge with swimming is that it seasonal for most of us. If you don't have a pool of your own, I'm sure you know where there is one. Make this part of your family's summer routine.

Bleachers

Take your kids to the high school football stadium in your town to walk or run up and down the bleachers. You can make it fun by taking turns hiding a prop or toy around the bleachers. Once one person finds the prop, he hides it somewhere else and the next person gets to look for it. It's a treasure hunt with sweat.

Playground equipment

Even the most addicted video gamer will have a great time on the jungle gym once he gets there. The trick is to get there. You can have a blast making up goofy games like "zombie tag."

Obstacle course

My children loved running an obstacle course when they were young. An obstacle course can be indoors or outdoors. If you're indoors, design a course around the house that includes over the couch, under the table and around carefully placed chairs.

Outdoors, you have a lot more options based on your environment. You can go under the picnic table, around the car, up the ladder and through the trees.

You might want to use a stopwatch and time each round through the obstacle course against your child's previous times. Your child will enjoy competing against himself. Siblings are already competitive enough though. Comparing your children's times will just cause animosity.

The classic childhood games
Tag, hide-and-seek, jump rope and hopscotch are fun regardless of your age. Get the whole family involved. These games are so much fun that it will be hard to stop once you get started.

The family fitness challenge
Devise a family fitness challenge that everyone can participate in once a week. It could be a one or two mile run, a mountain hike, a bike ride or a set of calisthenics upon which everyone has agreed in advance. Have your child help pick next week's family fitness challenge.

TV time
Once your children are old enough and you've taught them some basic exercise routines (push-ups, crunches, air squats, jump rope, etc.) Challenge them to exercise during every commercial of a one-hour program. It may not sound like much but it's amazing how many push-ups you can do in 16-minutes of commercials. If you're not convinced, try it for yourself first.

Household chores
Encourage your child to do his chores with vigor. Add some music to keep things alive. It's fun to mix exercises with the chores sometimes. For example, your child could vacuum for 2-minutes and then do 10-jumping jacks.

HEALTH PUZZLE PIECE 2

Get Enough Sleep

Is your child getting enough sleep? If not, she could be in trouble. Getting enough sleep is essential for your child's health. Sleep deprivation and its ensuing fatigue and exhaustion have serious consequences. They can weaken her immune system, sour her mood, modify her behavior and interfere with her ability to learn and develop in a healthy fashion.

How much sleep does your child need? Research shows that grade school age children need to sleep 10-11 hours each night. Middle and high school age children need 9-10 hours per night.

If your child is getting enough rest, then you can breeze through this chapter and move on to the next. But if she isn't, here are some guidelines to help you "guard" her sleep and protect her health.

Rest

Regeneration

Eagerness

Learning

Cheerfulness

Routine

Sleep

Health

Peace

Energy

DESCRIPTION

In today's fast-paced world, sleep is often treated as a low priority or an indulgence to be enjoyed only when there's time. For adults, dependence on caffeine and energy drinks is growing. For middle and high school aged children, unhealthy energy drinks are fast becoming the beverage of choice when they are with their friends.

Contrary to popular belief, sleep is essential to life. We have all performed poorly because we didn't get enough sleep. It's no different for your child. It's your job as a parent to guard your child's sleep. Otherwise, you are setting her up for failure. An exhausted child won't perform well at school, in sports or anywhere else. And she'll be more prone to get sick.

Children pay much closer attention to what we do than to what we say. Be a good example. Your child is already quite aware of your sleep habits. She seeks to emulate you. If you're not sleeping enough, it will be difficult for her to understand why she should sleep more. Also, if you are not sleeping enough, your home is more agitated, relationships are strained and it is much more difficult to relax and fall asleep. Such is the vicious cycle of sleep deprivation!

> *HEALTH PUZZLE PIECE 2 TOOL: Team up with your child to discuss the importance of sleep. Ask yourself what you need to change for your child to get enough rest. Then commit to making these changes. Readjust your routine to support your child getting enough sleep.*

TIPS:

Eliminate overstimulating activities such as exercise, loud music and television at least an hour before bedtime. These things tend to energize your child, making it difficult for her to drift off to sleep. Soothing music, reading or a bedtime story can really help set the mood for a good night's sleep.

Don't let your child sleep in too late on the weekends. Oversleeping on weekends makes it more difficult to get to bed at a decent hour on Sunday night. Going to bed too late on Sunday night can cause your child to start the week feeling tired, which makes it more difficult to catch up on sleep.

Encourage an afternoon power nap if necessary. If your child doesn't like naps and refuses to sleep, establish the habit of having her lie quietly for ten or fifteen minutes after school. This will make a huge difference in her mood and productivity all evening.

HEALTH PUZZLE PIECE 3

Eat Healthy Foods

People of all ages feel and function better when they're fit. Their self-esteem is higher, too. Part of being fit comes from eating right. No one wants to be overweight. Yet, the number of overweight and obese children (and adults) has risen to epidemic proportions in America. A lot of us were never taught how to eat to fuel our bodies. The wrong message is everywhere in the media. Calorie-rich but nutrient-poor food, which seems to be the normal fare most places, as well as the constant bombardment of different popular diet plans make it difficult to know just what to do.

Water

Natural

Fresh

Fruit

● *Delicious*

Vegetables

Healthy

Smaller

Slower

Mindful

Enjoyment

Choice

DESCRIPTION

Again, children look at what we do more than what we say. So it's really important that we set an example and team up with our children to eat healthy foods. It doesn't need to be complicated or difficult. In fact, you and your child can even have fun helping each other stick to these nine simple *Eat Healthy Guidelines*:

1. Stay hydrated.

2. Eat low on the food chain.

3. Eat fresh and unprocessed foods whenever possible.

4. Eat smaller portions.

5. Eat mindfully.

6. Eat more often.

7. Remember, "Being healthy and fit feels better than junk food tastes."

8. When it's junk food time, don't overdo it.

9. Eliminate something unhealthy from your diet.

Take it one step at a time. For example, you and your child could focus on just one of the following *Eat Healthy Guidelines* each week and make great progress.

EAT HEALTHY GUIDELINE 1

KEEP YOUR CHILD HYDRATED

Make sure that your child drinks enough water every day to keep his body working correctly. Did you know that dehydration is linked to fatigue, hunger and irritability? The next time your child feels grumpy, tired or very hungry, he might just be dehydrated.

How much water?
So how much water should your child drink everyday? A good rule of thumb is that both children and adults should drink half their weight in ounces everyday. That may seem like a lot but it's actually very easy to do. The key is to drink small amounts of water throughout the day.

H2O always the first choice
When your child is thirsty, water should always be your and her first choice. Of course, there may be times when she wants some other beverage such as soda or fruit juice. At the very least, beverages other than water should be enjoyed in moderation. When you do opt to give your child non-water beverages, it should be for their taste and not to quench her thirst.

What you should know about soda and other sugary drinks
• One can of soda (12 fl. oz.) contains 155 empty calories. Empty calories come from food that is high in sugar and fat but low in the nutrients that your child's body needs to stay healthy. One can of soda has the equivalent of 9-1/2 teaspoons of sugar. Are you kidding!

• That one can of soda causes a temporary spike in your blood sugar. While it does give you a temporary energy boost, you end up with far less energy than when you started once your blood sugar comes down.

• Excessive sugar from drinking soda not only leads to unnecessary weight gain, it can also lead to diabetes.

• There are 3,500 calories in a pound. In order to lose OR gain one pound, an individual must either subtract or add 3,500 calories from their diet. That equates to 22.5 sodas. If you drink one soda per day, you could gain as much as 16-pounds in one year. Or if you currently drink one soda everyday and decide to give it up, you could lose 16-pounds in one year.

• It takes about 23-minutes of walking to burn the calories in one can of soda.

• Diet sodas aren't much better. Although they do not have the calories of regular sodas, the chemically derived artificial sweeteners they contain (especially aspartame) may act as neurotoxins and have been linked to headaches, memory problems, anxiety, depression, skin irritations, joint pain and more.

- Fruit juice is high in sugar, too. Eat fruit instead of drinking fruit juice. If you do give your child fruit juice, keep it to a minimum and mix it with water.

Remember, water is the best thing for your child when she is thirsty. If she's going to drink anything else, it should be a small amount and for taste, not to quench her thirst.

> *EAT HEALTHY TOOL 1: Calculate how much water you and your child should drink every day by dividing each one of your weights in pounds by two.*

For example, if you weigh 160-pounds, you should drink 80-ounces of water every day. That equals ten 8-ounce glasses. Likewise, if your child weighs 80-pounds, then she should drink 40-ounces of water every day. That equals five 8-ounce glasses.

Team up with her. Help each other to remember to drink that number in ounces everyday for the next 7 days.

TIPS:

Start your day out right with your child. Together, drink at least 8-ounces of water first thing in the morning.

Have "special" water bottles that you and your child carry throughout the day and constantly sip from.

Choose water over sugary drinks.

EAT HEALTHY GUIDELINE 2

EAT LOW ON THE FOOD CHAIN

Make sure that you and your child eat low on the food chain. Eating low on the food chain means to eat lots of fruit and vegetables. This begins at the grocery store when you're deciding what to buy. Eating low on the food chain has many health benefits for you and your child:

* It helps to lower blood pressure.

* It reduces the risk of heart disease, stroke and some cancers.

* It lowers the risk of eye and digestive problems.

* It helps maintain healthy levels of blood sugar that can help keep appetite in check.

How much fruit and veggies?
There is a right amount of fruit and vegetables your child's body needs for optimum health. Nutritionists agree that your child needs five servings of fruit and vegetables every day to stay healthy. One serving is the amount of food that will fit in the palm of the eater's hand or about 1/2-cup. (Children have smaller hands than do adults, so a child's serving will be smaller than an adult's).

The beauty of vegetables
Most children like fruit better than vegetables but it's important to include vegetables. Vegetables are extremely high in vitamins and minerals and, generally, they are low in calories. Although fruit tends to be high in vitamins and minerals, it is also higher in sugar. It's nearly impossible to eat too many vegetables but this is not the case with fruit. For this reason we recommend a two to one ratio of vegetables to fruit.

Contrary to popular belief
Despite what you see in commercials, fruit juice, V-8 and other drinks made from fruits and vegetables aren't nearly as healthy for you or your child as the real thing. It's much better to eat fresh fruits and vegetables than it is to drink juice.

Orange juice vs. an orange

One 8-ounce glass of orange juice has well over 100-calories in it, the caloric equivalent of 2-1/2 oranges. With orange juice, your child doesn't get the benefits the actual orange has to offer, like roughage and additional vitamins and minerals contained in the roughage. Eating the actual fruit, rather than drinking the juice, will fill your child so he won't overeat.

> *EAT HEALTHY TOOL 2: Team up with your child to eat a minimum of 5 servings of fresh fruits and vegetables everyday with at least 3 of the servings coming from vegetables. Drinks do not count. It has to be the real thing.*

TIPS:

Fresh or frozen fruit and vegetables are always better than canned or overcooked.

Grocery shop with your child and play the game, *This-or-That?* Compare two items and ask your child, *This or that?* to choose the healthier option. You can do this when you are eating out, too.

EAT HEALTHY GUIDELINE 3

EAT FRESH AND UNPROCESSED FOODS
WHENEVER POSSIBLE

Our bodies thrive on natural, fresh foods. There's no doubt about it! It's better to eat fresh and unprocessed (natural foods) whenever possible. Processed food is food that has been chemically altered with additives, such as flavor enhancers, binders, colors, fillers, preservatives, stabilizers, emulsifiers, etc. Generally, if any of the ingredients in food aren't "natural," it can be considered to be processed.

There is a wide range of processed foods. Extremely processed foods (think "Twinkies") aren't even real food. They are edible food-like substances with no nutritional value and potentially harmful effects.

Not all processed food is bad
Processing has made the world's food supply much safer to eat and has made the storage of food a much healthier and more viable option. Processing kills pathogens and extends the shelf life of food. If there were a food shortage or, even a famine, processed food items would remain edible and could keep you alive a lot longer than raw food which would rot within a few days.

The benefits of fresh and natural foods
Despite the benefits of processed food, a diet consisting exclusively of processed foods leads to disease. Fresh and unprocessed foods contain beneficial enzymes and nutrients that are destroyed through processing.

A pill or nutritional supplement won't cut it
Just because a pill contains the "nutrients" of a whole shopping list of vegetables and fruit, it doesn't mean that our bodies will receive the same benefit as we would from eating the vegetables and fruit themselves. The nutrients, enzymes and other components of the foods we eat work synergistically. No one knows how well they work when these components are isolated from each other or when we ingest synthetic versions.

Choosing wisely
How can we realistically minimize the amount of processed food that our children consume? By making healthy decisions at the grocery store, in restaurants and at home. For example, we can offer our children:

* An apple instead of applesauce or apple juice

* Grape Nuts instead of Lucky Charms

* A baked potato or a salad instead of French fries

* Real food like oatmeal, 100% whole grain bread, pasta, beans and legumes (and, of course, fresh fruits and vegetables)

EAT HEALTHY TOOL 3: Team up with your child to replace as many white flour products with whole grain products as possible. Make sure the label reads "100% Whole Wheat" or "100% Multi-Grain," not just "Wheat" or "Multi-Grain."

Replace white rice with brown rice.

Replace all over-processed breakfast cereal with a more natural, healthy choice.

Eat fruit instead of drinking fruit juice. If you want juice, try squeezing your own from fresh fruit.

TIPS:

Eliminate or minimize the use of high calorie condiments like butter and margarine, mayonnaise, BBQ Sauce, etc.

Use lemon or oil and vinegar sparingly on your salad instead of ranch and other "heavy" salad dressings.

Start looking at the ingredients listed on food labels and try to buy foods with fewer ingredients listed.

Make an extra effort to minimize foods that have lots of hard to pronounce, scientific names in their lists of ingredients.

Avoid foods that contain high fructose corn syrup and partially hydrogenated vegetable oil (trans fat).

EAT HEALTHY GUIDELINE 4

EAT SMALLER PORTIONS

Most of us are in the habit of eating until we feel full but science has proven time and time again that systematic undereating prolongs life. The idea is not to deprive yourself, but to eat a little less than you might be used to. It really isn't that difficult. All you have to do is to make a conscious effort to take smaller portions.

Hari Hachi Bu

One of the healthiest countries in the world is Okinawa. The traditional Okinawan diet consists almost exclusively of fresh, unprocessed foods. But that is not the only reason for their high level of health. The Okinawans have the saying, "Hari Hachi Bu," which means "80% full." The idea is that you never stuff yourself. Instead of eating until you're full, you eat until you are not hungry. This takes practice and discipline but the benefits are significant.

If you have a child who doesn't eat enough, then you can apply the tool below to eating smaller portions of desserts and junk food.

EAT HEALTHY TOOL 4: Team up with your child to make a conscious effort to eat a bit less at every meal. This doesn't apply to fruits and vegetables. Don't skimp on those. Eating a little bit less at every meal applies to food like macaroni and cheese, French fries, potato chips, ice cream, cookies, crackers and sugary cereal. Remember, instead of eating until you are full, eat until you are no longer hungry.

TIPS:

Try using a smaller plate for all your meals. This makes it seem like there is more food on the plate. Research shows us that by doing this you will automatically eat less.

Most entrées at restaurants are oversized. Try sharing one entrée with someone else or eating only half and taking the rest to go.

Replace large smoothies with small ones.

Replace a 12-inch sandwich with a 6-inch, etc.

EAT HEALTHY GUIDELINE 5

EAT MINDFULLY

Teach your child to eat mindfully. What is mindful eating? To eat mindfully is to eat in a calm, slow and deliberate way.

Eat less and enjoy it more.
You have practiced mindful eating plenty of times in the past (perhaps without even knowing it). For example, have you ever been looking forward to a big slice of chocolate cake only to find out that there was only a small sliver left? You probably didn't devour it in one quick bite. More likely, you ate it in small pieces and tried to enjoy every crumb. That's mindful eating. The bottom line is that, when you eat mindfully, you will find yourself eating less and enjoying it more.

Multi-tasking vs. mindful eating
In today's busy world, many Americans often multitask by eating while they do other activities. How many times have we eaten while driving, watching TV, working, etc.? Although we think that we are making good use of our time, eating on the run can actually work against us.

When we eat while focusing on another activity we tend to eat too fast and overeat. Thoroughly chewing your food increases your body's ability to digest effectively and it also allows you to feel satiated sooner. When you eat too fast the feeling of being full doesn't kick in until after you've eaten way too much. When you slow down the meal you feel satisfied more quickly.

Also, when we're not paying attention to what we're eating we tend to make less healthy food choices. And finally, we miss out on the sheer enjoyment of our meal!

EAT HEALTHY TOOL 5: Team up with your child to make a conscious effort to eat at least one meal each day together mindfully from start to finish. It can be breakfast, lunch or dinner—whichever one works best for you—but it has to be at least one meal per day.

With your other meals, team up with your child to make sure you chew the first three bites in a slow, mindful fashion. For example instead of chewing a bite ten times, try chewing it twenty-five times. If you can do this with more than three bites, that's great! But, at the very least, eat the first three bites mindfully.

TIPS:

Make sure that you have no distractions during your meals other than good conversation with friends and family.

Turn off the TV, put down the book and step away from the computer when it's time to eat.

Make a conscious effort to try to chew every bite more thoroughly.

To maximize your mealtime enjoyment, make your environment as peaceful and attractive as possible. Clear the table of clutter. Use tableware that looks and feels good. Make sure your food is presented in an attractive and pleasing way. Slow down the meal. Enjoy it. You'll be glad you did.

EAT HEALTHY GUIDELINE 6

EAT MORE OFTEN

There are many benefits to eating several small meals each day, rather than a few larger meals. Children are inclined to do this naturally. Once you get used to it, you'll like it, too.

Five or six smaller meals
The goal is to eat the same amount you normally would in a day but as smaller meals more often. For example, enjoy five or six smaller meals in a

day instead of three larger ones. Remember that, *a meal* does not refer to a 3-course banquet. We're referring to breakfast, lunch and dinner just like you normally have but with smaller portions—and then adding two or three smaller meals in between.

Skipping meals doesn't work for weight loss

People (and often teenagers) who are trying to lose weight will often skip meals but it doesn't work like that. The assumption is that consuming fewer calories results in weight loss but the opposite is true. When you skip a meal your body goes into starvation mode. This basically means that your metabolism slows down and your body tries to retain every calorie it can in the form of fat. Actually, by skipping meals you will get the exact results you were trying to avoid.

Also, your feeling of hunger is exaggerated when you skip meals. When this happens you feel ravenous, lose your self-control and are very likely to end up eating anything and everything put in front of you. When you skip meals, you usually end up consuming more calories than you would by eating smaller meals throughout the day.

Eating more often can help you lose weight

Eat less food more often throughout the day sends your body a clear signal to keep the metabolism moving fast because the next meal is just around the corner. Also, because the next meal is coming up soon, you and your child won't feel quite as hungry. You will be able to exercise better self-control and make better choices.

EAT HEALTHY TOOL 6: Team up with your child to eat 5-6 smaller, healthy meals a day.

TIPS:

The additional meals might consist of low-fat yogurt and an apple, maybe some carrot sticks and a handful of nuts or a bowl of oatmeal and a banana. It really helps to have these ingredients on hand.

EAT HEALTHY GUIDELINE 7

REMEMBER THAT BEING HEALTHY AND FIT FEELS BETTER THAN ANY JUNK FOOD TASTES

The American culture is a junk food culture. Junk food is readily available to our children just about everywhere. Junk food is often used as a reward for achievements and to celebrate special occasions in school. In the high school cafeteria, there is a wide selection of junk food. Junk food is everywhere.

As you and your child strive to eat mindfully to be healthy, it's important she does not feel deprived when you say, "No," to junk food. Social situations are even tougher where she needs to make the decision herself. (Even though we know that junk food isn't good for us we're still tempted.)

So how do you help your child to deal with all the temptation? And how do you help her not feel deprived? Team up with her to remind one another that the feeling you get from being healthy and fit feels a lot better than any junk food tastes. Junk food just isn't worth it.

See through the ruse
The only benefit to junk food is its taste. And the taste experience lasts only the length of time it takes to eat it. Then it's over. What's left? Feeling bloated, weight gain, upset stomach, heartburn and fatigue. We've been programmed by junk food manufacturers to believe that we crave it and that it will satisfy us somehow, when the truth is that it only makes us feel unhealthy. Remember that no one ever regrets the junk food he didn't eat.

Develop a game plan
It helps to be prepared for the inevitable temptations that arise. Develop a game plan. Take some time to affirm with your child just how great you'll both feel knowing that you and she have the strength to resist temptation … that resisting junk food will make you both feel stronger, rather than "deprived." Talk about how good it will feel to make a healthy choice. Every time you or your child triumph over temptation you'll both be empowered. The more you practice the easier it will get to resist junk food.

> *EAT HEALTHY TOOL 7: Team up with your child to find some of her favorite, unhealthy junk food choices (candy, soda, cake, chips, Cheetos, etc.) and take a close look at them with her. Then imagine together. Instead of looking at the junk food with desire, imagine all of the extra sugar, fat and calories it has. Imagine how good you are going to feel when you don't give into the temptation. Say aloud with your child, "Being healthy and fit feels better than that junk food tastes."*

TIPS:

Remember that whenever the temptation to eat junk food occurs your and your child's response can be to say to yourselves, "Being healthy and fit feels better than that junk food tastes."

EAT HEALTHY GUIDELINE 8

DON'T OVERDO IT WHEN IT'S JUNK FOOD TIME

Being a healthy eater does not mean that your child must never again enjoy tasty treats that may not be good for him. That would be no fun! In fact, it's important for your child to enjoy his favorite foods occasionally, even if they aren't healthy.

The trick is not to overindulge. For example, if your child likes candy he should enjoy it from time to time. Just be sure that he enjoys it less often and in smaller portions. As we've discussed earlier, your child will probably enjoy a smaller portion more because he is more likely to be mindful and appreciative of every bite.

A clear plan of action

To help your child refrain from overindulging, you'll need a clear plan ahead of time. One approach is to set aside one day each week for junk food. For example, perhaps you and your child decide to eat junk food only from Saturday evening to Sunday evening. This would mean that during the rest of the week your child doesn't eat that chocolate cake. Most likely, this approach will give your child the willpower he needs to resist junk food for the rest of the week because, in the back of his mind, he knows that he can look forward to enjoying a small portion on the upcoming weekend.

Another strategy is to pick one time everyday when you are going to allow your child to have a small portion of his favorite junk food. Be sure stick to the plan. And don't forget the word "small." This is crucial to your long-term success.

Completely guilt-free
When you and your child are following a predetermined plan and it is time to enjoy a little junk food, don't feel guilty. Instead, enjoy yourself and move on.

EAT HEALTHY TOOL 8: Team up with your child to pick one of two choices. The first choice is to not eat any junk food except on your predetermined junk food day.

The second choice is to reduce the amount of junk food your child eats everyday by at least half. It's important that it is less than half of what he currently eats. Otherwise there will be no challenge.

TIP:

Remember that you can eat anything you want within reason once in awhile but not everything you want at any time.

EAT HEALTHY GUIDELINE 9

ELIMINATE SOMETHING UNHEALTHY FROM YOUR DIET

We've discussed several different strategies that are extremely effective in helping your child to overcome unhealthy eating habits. But in extreme cases, there are times when you need to swing the pendulum far to one side to regain control.

The challenge is to eliminate something unhealthy from her diet. Imagine that she has developed a habit of drinking a 2-liter bottle of soda each day. Just cutting down on such an excessive amount might not be enough. Drinking less soda everyday might just make her desire for it increase. She could feel deprived and want more. By teaming up with your child to eliminate soda completely it will no longer be such a big deal. And when she does get it in small amounts it will be a treat.

Your child will feel stronger by voluntarily making the decision to eliminate soda from her diet for a week. There is an amazing sense of power that she will feel when she commits to eliminating something unhealthy from her diet and then successfully sticks to her commitment. She will gain a healthy sense of control with her diet.

The habit of drinking or eating something unhealthy will be easier to beat if you replace the unhealthy food with something healthy in order to "fill the void." For example, if your child is used to eating an unhealthy food before bed every evening she might eat an apple at that time. This will make the process of eliminating the unhealthy food that much easier.

EAT HEALTHY TOOL 9: Team up with your child to find something in each of your individual diets that is unhealthy and completely eliminate it for the next seven days. At the end of the week you and your child can reevaluate. If you and your child find that it was easier than you thought, you might choose to reduce the unhealthy foods or completely eliminate them from your diet as you go forward.

TIP:

Remember you and your child don't have to pick from the junk food list. There are probably lots of things that you eat during breakfast, lunch or dinner that you would be better off without. You might consider eliminating something like bacon, hamburgers, sour cream or mayonnaise. Try to stretch yourself. It's only for a week so pick something challenging.

SECTION 3
Family Safety Principles

INTRODUCTION

Although there is a lot of violence in modern society there is plenty we can do to minimize the odds of it happening to our children. Can a man take every precaution possible to keep his family safe and still have his child suffer violence? Of course. However, with the right preparation, the right training and the right mindset, the odds will be strongly stacked in your child's favor.

An ounce of prevention is worth a pound of cure certainly applies to keeping our families safe. These *Family Safety Principles* will help you train your child in strategic self-defense to feel more confident and empowered. Your child will communicate more confidence in the way she carries herself. Because bullies and predators usually approach children who appear vulnerable, hesitant or fearful, they will be less likely to single out your confident, empowered child.

As fathers we are genetically wired to be the protectors of our family. There are conflicting theories as to when parents should begin to discuss real-world dangers with their children or if the topic should be broached at all.

Some parents feel that ignorance is bliss. They are determined to shield their children from knowing about the dangers in the world as long as possible. Other parents feel it is important to develop street-smarts from a young age so no one takes advantage of their children.

My take is that real-world dangers need to be discussed but that the discussion should be age-appropriate and introduced over time.

Empowerment vs. fear-based education

The overriding theme should be empowerment-based education not fear-based education. If you keep your child in the dark regarding safety issues, she can grow up naïve and be easy prey for predators. Whereas, if your consistent message is to "beware of strangers because there are a lot of bad people out there that want to hurt you," your child could grow up being overly fearful. This fear does not make your child safer. In fact, being overly fearful puts her more at risk.

Calm and age appropriate discussion

The key is to discuss real-world, age-appropriate dangers in a calm, matter-of-fact fashion. Explain to your child that while there are bad guys out there, the majority of people they meet are good—but to be safe, there are certain guidelines that they should always follow.

A strategic view with tactical strategies
Family Safety Principles will give you a high-level, strategic view with tactical strategies that you can share and practice with your children. Just like everything else, discussing safety with your child needs to be an ongoing dialogue ... not a one-time event.

FAMILY SAFETY PRINCIPLE 1

Create Safe Habits

While most of us know how to live a safe life, we're not always aware of what we know. As dads it is important to be conscious of what we know and to teach our children to be mindful, too. Awareness is the first step to safety.

To keep your family safe doesn't require that you lock them in the house and not let them out. On the contrary! Once you're aware of what you know about staying safe and put this simple knowledge into action you will be giving your family more freedom than ever.

You create safe habits by doing what you know you should do. You help your child to create safe habits by teaching her to avoid potentially dangerous situations in the first place.

Knowledge

Safety

Wisdom

Protection

Intelligence

DESCRIPTION

Years ago, a man walked into my martial arts school to ask about lessons. He was sporting a black eye, stitches and a fat lip. It was pretty obvious that he'd been in a fight and wanted to learn to protect himself.

He told me quite candidly that he needed to learn self-defense. When I asked him why, he said that every time he went into this certain bar, he got into a fight. I responded, half jokingly, by telling him not to go to the bar in the first place. He literally slapped himself on the forehead and with a startled look said, "I never thought of that. What a great idea!" To me, this seemed obvious but, until I mentioned it, he had never thought of avoiding the potential for danger.

You'll be surprised how much you know already about safe habits. The following examples illustrate this point:

- Wear a seat belt

- Lock the car and house doors

- Get cash inside a store, not at an outside automated teller

- Fill up on gas in a good area of town during the day

- Shop with a friend

- Park in well-lit areas

- When shopping, park as close as possible to the store with your car door facing the store

Pretty basic stuff that every adult should know, right? Do you follow these rules? Remember that creating safe habits doesn't mean you are being paranoid but that you are being smart and stacking the odds for safety in your favor.

Once you realize how much about safety you already know and recommit yourself to practicing safe habits, teach your child to do the same thing. Again, teaching your child to create safe habits requires an ongoing conversation. A one-time discussion isn't enough. Discuss the importance of avoiding potentially dangerous situations with your child frequently. The Socratic method works best. Teach your child by asking questions rather than by lecturing her.

FAMILY SAFETY PRINCIPLE TOOL 1:
Here's the big question—What potentially dangerous situations do you need to keep your child from getting into in the first place? Ask your child to name some dangerous situations that she should avoid. Your questions can guide her to discover the following scenarios and more.

- Busy street

- Construction site

- River

- School bully

- Talking with a grown-up she doesn't know when her parents aren't around

Next, ask your child why she should avoid those situations and what the potential dangers are. Remember, don't scare her. Empower her. Remind her that if she creates safe habits, chances are, that she will be just fine.

TIP:

Create a curfew and stick with it unwaveringly. Nothing good happens after curfew.

FAMILY SAFETY PRINCIPLE 2

Be aware but not on guard

Being aware of potentially dangerous situations is not the same as being on guard. Being aware means to pay attention to what is going on around you, to exercise your peripheral vision to take in the details of your surroundings and to notice when something is not quite right or is very wrong.

Awareness

Responsiveness

Vision

Alertness

Attention

DESCRIPTION

Teaching our children to be aware should be empowering not scary. Arm your child with the gift of awareness. Discuss being aware of dangerous situations frequently. The possible dangerous scenarios will change as your child grows. Continue the dialogue throughout your child's growing years.

To be aware is neither to be on guard or its opposite, to be naive. Being aware is a lot like being a good driver. A good driver sees the big picture rather than narrowing his focus to one aspect of driving. Through relaxed, soft concentration a skilled driver puts his attention wherever it is most needed while still keeping his eye on the road and his surroundings.

An experienced driver neither expects to get into an accident nor does he rule out the possibility of an accident. He follows the rules of the road and doesn't overreact or underreact to his environment. If something were to occur on the road, the defensive driver trusts his instinct and skills to respond correctly.

Similar to the defensive driver, you can teach your child to be aware of his surroundings but not be excessively fearful. With this mindset, he can safely go about his business. He can be confident that, when something comes up that needs his immediate attention, his intuition will let him know.

We've all seen both on guard and naive drivers. They're scary! They overcompensate, overreact or neglect to respond to the conditions of the road. They create dangerous situations.

FAMILY SAFETY PRINCIPLE TOOL 2: Once you are aware of how you are regarding safety, you can adjust it (if needed) to help your child be healthily aware but not on guard. Ask yourself where you fall on the safety scale:

- Are you more cautious and fearful than you should be? (Paranoid)

- Are you not cautious enough? (Naïve)

- Are you aware but relatively free from over-worrying?

Your answer is important because your child will adopt a similar mindset. Our children imitate how we are, as well as what we do. Also, your answer will make you aware of any changes you need to make regarding how you teach your child to drive his own life safely.

This awareness extends beyond being aware of potentially dangerous situations to being aware of others' goodness and the beauty of life, too. Team up with your child to notice how many good things are happening—acts of kindness, creativity, the beauty of nature, etc.

FAMILY SAFETY PRINCIPLE 3

Trust your intuition

We all have had gut feelings about a person, place or event which we should have heeded but didn't. Fortunately, most of these incidents were probably not life threatening. Can you think of a time when your instincts didn't seem logical but were absolutely correct? Of course you can. We've all had this experience.

Intuition

Instinct

Listening

Responsiveness

Honor

DESCRIPTION

Our intuition is always right in two important ways. It's always in response to something. And it always has our best interest in mind.

Listening to your intuition seems simple but it isn't always easy. As a matter of fact, many of us have been taught to ignore or stifle our intuition. There is often no logical explanation for what intuition is guiding us to do. We're used to feeling that we have to substantiate our decisions with hard facts for them to be viable. But intuition doesn't work that way. It's usually only after we listen or don't listen to it that we see exactly why our instincts made sense. If you have been taught to stifle your intuition then you're in danger of teaching your child to stifle her intuition and this puts her in danger.

Please note that your *intuition* or *instinct* is your innate knowing, your awareness on a deep level that keeps you and your child safe. Intuition is very different than are *triggers*. Triggers are incidents to which you have a deep psychological, emotional and, sometimes, physical reaction, based on your past. Reacting to triggers usually creates dangerous situations, whereas listening to intuition protects us from danger.

It is important that we teach our children to honor their feelings about circumstances and people. Listen to your child with your full attention. Encourage your child to talk about it. If someone makes your child feel uncomfortable, tell her that you're glad she told you and that you want her to bring these things to your attention.

FAMILY SAFETY PRINCIPLE TOOL 3: Make a game of honing your child's intuition by constantly looking for teachable moments. Movies, stories and even television shows can be full of great lessons that you can discuss with your child. Each day holds many real-life opportunities to teach your child to trust her intuition, too. The key is to ask your child frequently what she observes about other families, people and situations. Not only will she love the fact that you're curious about what she sees and the way she sees it, you'll be able to help her hone her intuition and to validate it with a few simple questions about her feelings and observations.

A Dad's Toolbox for Better Parenting

FAMILY SAFETY PRINCIPLE 4

Take immediate action.

Teach your child to be proactive under pressure and take immediate action. Usually this action is to leave the scene of trouble immediately.

Action

Immediacy

Bolt

Run

DESCRIPTION

Let's imagine the worst-case scenario for a moment. Your child finds himself confronted with a hostile situation. He has tried to diffuse the situation by practicing safe habits and being aware of his surroundings but still hasn't been able to avoid a confrontation. Aggressive action must be taken immediately. He should leave the scene quickly, if at all possible.

Leaving a dangerous situation quickly is called "bolt and run." The idea behind bolt and run is to avoid putting yourself in a situation worse than the one you're already in.

Although there are times when your child needs to stand up for himself, dangerous situations are not those times. When it comes to imminent danger, your child needs to know how to bolt and run. It's survival at that point.

In law enforcement, *Crime Scene 1* is where the incident starts. And *Crime Scene 2* is wherever it ends up. *Crime Scene 2* is always worse than *Crime Scene 1*. Leaving the scene quickly will help your child remove himself from danger and avoid being a victim in *Crime Scene 2*.

> *FAMILY SAFETY PRINCIPLE TOOL 4: Role-play with your child by setting up different scenarios to act out. Have him help choose the scenarios. For example, you can pretend to be a strange adult who approaches him at the park and forcefully says, "Hey kid, come here right now."*

A Dad's Toolbox for Better Parenting

FAMILY SAFETY PRINCIPLE 5

Learn from your and others' experiences

We're all human and we all make mistakes. No one is perfect. But as long as we approach life as learners, we'll keep progressing. The trick is to teach your child to learn from her and others' mistakes and not repeat them.

Progress

Learn

Examine

Observe

Evaluate

Practice

Implement

Teach

DESCRIPTION

Learning from history keeps us from repeating it. Take a moment to think of times in the past when you unnecessarily put your safety at risk. What can you learn from this experience? How could you have handled this situation better? What steps can you take to ensure that this will not happen to you again? This will help you examine your mistakes in a new light ... to learn from them. Then you'll be able to do this with your child.

It's important to remember that self-defense defies logic. Everyday someone somewhere effectively diffuses a potentially dangerous situation. Everyday someone somewhere effectively fights off and breaks free from a violent attack. How? She has what is referred to as *the not-me mindset*. She has decided that she will not become a victim. This is what we want to try to instill in our children as we teach them simple self-defense strategies, including learning from their and others' mistakes.

FAMILY SAFETY PRINCIPLE TOOL 5: Ask your child to think of times when she put her own safety at risk unnecessarily. What did she learn from this experience? How could she have handled this situation better? What steps can she take to make sure that this won't happen again? Also, anytime you hear of something negative happening to someone else ask your child (if the topic is age-appropriate), "How could this have been avoided?"

You may not always come up with clear and decisive answers to every question. By having this dialogue frequently you help your child pick up clear, useable distinctions that can help her to respond better in the future. You are teaching her critical thinking or how to have the not-me or "safety" mindset.

A Dad's Toolbox for Better Parenting

FAMILY SAFETY PRINCIPLE 6

Communicate with confidence

The FBI did a study several years ago entitled, *The Three Stages of Assault*. In this study, the FBI uncovered the fact that most predators follow a basic pattern of attack.

First they "select" a victim.

Next, they "test" the victim for perceived vulnerability.

Finally, they "commit" the physical assault.

With this in mind, the first step is to figure out how to minimize the risk of your child being selected in the first place. We already know that teaching our children to practice safe habits is the number one most important thing we can do to help them stay safe. But safe habits are not enough in and of themselves

Inevitably, there will be times when your child's path might cross that of a predator. For this reason, you need to teach him how to develop the habit of communicating confidence in all of his actions even when he doesn't feel confident. Be aware that the average bad guy doesn't have a back-up plan but he does have an alternate victim. By teaching your child to communicate more confidently you dramatically reduce his chances of being selected as a potential victim in the first place.

Super Kid

Eye Contact

Body Language

Voice

Confidence

Power

Strength

Action

Safety

DESCRIPTION

There is probably nothing more important for your child's safety than teaching him to carry himself with confidence. The three primary indicators of confidence are:

Body Language
Body language can either send the message that you're likely to be a passive, easy target or it can tell a potential attacker that he'd be better off picking someone else.

Eye Contact
Making eye contact sends the message that you're aware that the predator is there and that you're not likely to be a good target.

Tonality
The third step is Tonality. It isn't *what* you say, it's *how* you say it. Saying "Back off!" with authority has much more impact that saying it in a weak voice.

Assertive body posture, making eye contact and using strong tonality combine to make a strong statement to the attacker that he would be better off choosing someone else.

FAMILY SAFETY PRINCIPLE TOOL 6: Team up with your child to practice the PushoverKid/SuperKid drill. First have him stand with slouched shoulders, his head down and his eyes looking towards the floor. This is PushoverKid. Ask him how he feels when he stands like that. Chances are that he'll tell you that he doesn't feel very good or confident.

Next have him pull his shoulders back and puff out his chest, bring his head up and chin in and have him make clear eye contact straight at you. This is SuperKid. To dramatize the effect even more, have him ball his hands into fists and rest them on his hips just like Superman. Ask him how he feels then. Chances are that he'll feel much more empowered. Although this is an exaggeration, it gets the point across—appearing and acting confident is the first step to becoming more confident.

FAMILY SAFETY PRINCIPLE 7

Follow the five steps of bully prevention

Bullying has always been a serious issue for children. It is estimated that nearly 40% of children have reported bullying and a large percentage of those children say it happens everyday. What can we do to minimize the chances of our children being bullied? First and foremost, teach your child to ask an adult for help when she needs it. And if the problem is ongoing, your child can ask for help in advance of the actual bullying to prevent the situation from unfolding in a negative way.

Happy
Healthy
Mind
Words
Legs
Ask
Defend

DESCRIPTION

Before we get into specific strategies to prevent bullying, let's not forget that by simply following the guidelines laid out to you in *Parenting Guidelines* and *The Health Puzzle* you will be going a long way to keeping your child safe from being a target of bullying.

This is because healthy children brought up in a loving atmosphere who have a high level of self-esteem are naturally less likely to be bullied in the first place. It is important that your child feels comfortable talking to you about anything. Frequently remind her that she can talk to you about anything. When she does want to talk to you about a sensitive issue make sure not to jump all over her or to discount her feelings. Otherwise she'll quit talking to you about sensitive subjects. Remember that as an adult, someone calling your child a name might seem trivial but it can be traumatic. Just being there to listen will go a long way in keeping your relationship strong with your child.

The traditional, misguided way of dealing with a bully is to bring your child into the backyard to teach her how to punch. Although there is a lot of value in teaching your child actual self-defense skills, dealing with a bully involves a lot more than knowing how to throw a right cross.

In our martial arts schools, we teach the five steps of bully prevention:

- Use your mind.
- Use your words.
- Use your legs.
- Ask for help.
- Defend yourself.

Use your mind. Teach your child to think ahead about all the things she can do to stay safe.

Use your words. Teach your child to use her words to talk her way out of trouble. In many cases, responding to a bully with eye contact and a confident voice takes some of the wind out of the bully's sails. After all, it's no fun bullying someone who won't let you push her around or who does not seem to be bothered by it.

Use your legs. Teach your child to walk (or run) away from trouble when words aren't working. This applies any time she is confronted by someone who is being mean to her and whom she doesn't know, and who she'll probably never see again. She could be at a park, mall, fair, sports field, etc. When using her words isn't working and she feels a fight coming on—and if she feels that she can get away—then she should get away ... even RUN!

Ask for help. Teach your child that it is okay to ask for help if she is afraid or feels threatened. This is very important. Most kids don't want to be a tattletale. They are afraid that if they tell a parent or teacher about a bully or troublemaker that the other kids will make fun of them. Asking for help in advance might be the solution. Remind your child frequently that it is okay to ask for help. Assure her that her safety is important to you and her teachers.

Defend yourself. Teach your child that no one has the right to physically harm her. If she has had done everything within her power to avoid a confrontation, then she has the right to defend herself. Please understand that it's important to teach your child to be 100% against fighting. But if her back is against the wall and she has no choice, then your child should be 100% for defending herself.

It's amazing to me that just the simple act of being prepared to defend yourself can often keep the fight from ever happening. In martial arts we call it *practice the fight so that you don't have to.*

FAMILY SAFETY PRINCIPLE TOOL 7: Have you child memorize the Five Steps of Bully Prevention by having her hold out her hand with her fingers spread. As she recites each rule, she brings one finger in slowly to make a fist. As she finishes the fifth step and closes her hand into a complete fist, have her say loudly, "Defend yourself!" and punch into the air.

FAMILY SAFETY PRINCIPLE 8

Dispel the myth of not talking to strangers

Teaching your child not to talk to strangers is a completely abstract concept that is difficult for your child to understand because the child gets mixed messages. For example, if a woman in the grocery store checkout line asks your daughter for her name and she doesn't reply, you might chastise your daughter for being rude and ask her to tell the nice lady her name.

Wisdom

Awareness

Care

Goodness

DESCRIPTION

I've given literally hundreds of school talks on this subject and am amazed at what I hear from students when I ask them what a stranger looks like. Generally speaking, children describe a stranger as someone who is big and scary, wears sunglasses and has a lot of tattoos and a beard.

I tell the kids that a stranger is simply someone that they don't know until their parents introduce them. Then I remind them that most strangers are good people who have no interest in harming them. But, unfortunately, there are a few individuals who aren't good people. So we need to take certain precautions. I also tell them that there is a difference between *niceness* and *goodness*. Just because somebody is *nice* to you doesn't necessarily mean that he's a *good* person.

> *FAMILY SAFETY PRINCIPLE TOOL 8: Team up with your child to help her hone her instincts about who she should and should not talk to by discussing real-life situations. Asking your child questions will help her understand what degree of interaction is appropriate with an adult. For example, after you walk out of the grocery store where you had your child introduce herself to the person in front of you, you can ask her, "That was a nice man, wasn't he? If I weren't around and he asked you to go somewhere with him, would you do it? Why not?"*

A Dad's Toolbox for Better Parenting

FAMILY SAFETY PRINCIPLE 9

Know who to ask for help

The thought of getting lost is scary for people of all ages. It can be especially frightening for children. Many parents give their children the well-intended advice, "Don't talk to strangers." However, the whole concept of strangers is confusing and misleading for your child.

As we discussed in *Family Safety Principle 8*, a stranger is simply someone whom your child doesn't know until you have introduced him. What does your child do if he's lost or separated from the family if he is not to talk to strangers? He'll withdraw and become more frightened and confused if he is afraid to ask for help. It is a known fact that predators look for lost, lonely, confused or weaker victims.

Ask

Moms

Grandmas

Uniforms

Workers

DESCRIPTION

If your child is lost or needs help for some reason, should he wait for somebody to come up to him to see if he needs help? Or should he ask someone for help? Most definitely, teach your child to ask for help.

Remember that the odds of your child approaching a predator to ask for help are pretty rare. Conversely, the odds of a predator approaching your child if he appears lost are much greater. For this reason, it's crucial to teach your child to approach someone to ask for help when he is lost or needs help. But who?

Let's assume there are lots of grown-ups around but he doesn't know any of them and there are no law officers to be seen. Who should he ask?

Moms with children should be his first choice. Their strong maternal instinct kicks in immediately as they picture their own children lost. Usually, a mom will do everything in her power to help your child.

Next on the list is someone that looks like a grandma for the same reasons. After that, any person in uniform ... the UPS person, mail carrier ... pretty much anyone in uniform will do. And if your child can't find anybody who fits the above descriptions, he should look for someone working. Also, remind your child to stay put. Wandering off to look for you or his mom will only confuse him and make him more difficult to find.

Teaching your child to be assertive and to approach adults is very empowering and can go a long way towards making him feel more confident.

FAMILY SAFETY PRINCIPLE TOOL 9: When you're out and about with your child, ask your child to be aware of the people around him and choose someone he'd ask for help. Do it often and in many different types of places. And team up with your child to practice actually approaching an adult he doesn't know.

GAME 1—Whom should I ask for help? Sit in the park with your child and have him tell you about all the people he sees. Ask him which person he would approach for help and why. If he gets it right, let him know. If he could have made a better selection, tell him why and start over again.

GAME 2—Excuse me, do you have the time? Go to a public place someplace where there are a lot of people. Have your child pick out someone he feels comfortable approaching. Have him walk up to that person and simply ask for the time.

FAMILY SAFETY PRINCIPLE 10

When in doubt, get out

Every responsible parent tries to teach his child good manners. We teach our children to be especially polite to grown-ups. We teach them to follow the rules, listen to their teachers and obey authority. While these are all important things, we should also teach them that, if they ever feel uncomfortable around an adult, it's okay to risk offending the adult. Teach them that, when in doubt, get out! Even if it might offend someone.

Intuition

Action

Safety

Back off

Get Away

Leave

DESCRIPTION

Teach your child that her safety is more important than any adult's feelings. Your child should be taught never to worry about hurting someone's feelings if she feels that her safety is at risk. Better to risk offending an adult by telling him to back off or get away—even if it becomes clear later on that the adult had no ill intent—than it is to go along with an adult's seemingly innocent request because she didn't want to hurt his feelings. When in doubt, get out!

Teach your child that "when in doubt, get out" means that she always trusts her intuition ... that intuition is:

- that feeling she gets about places or people that she just can't quite explain.

- when someone gives her the creeps or when being somewhere makes her feel uncomfortable.

- her radar that warns and protects her from danger.

Teach her that she should always listen to her intuition. This means that if she ever feels uncomfortable with someone or someplace she should leave and find help, even if it hurts another's feelings. Have an ongoing dialogue about intuition and the importance of listening to it. Praise your child when you see her listening to her intuition. Frequently remind your child that it's okay to risk hurting people's feelings if it means keeping herself safe.

FAMILY SAFETY PRINCIPLE TOOL 10: Teach your child the statement, "My safety is more important than their feelings." Have your child say, "My safety is more important than their feelings," aloud and with confidence again and again. Have your child yell it. Join in. Yell with your child, "My safety is more important than their feelings!" Present different scenarios and play-practice listening to intuition, leaving and getting help with your child.

A Dad's Toolbox for Better Parenting

FAMILY SAFETY PRINCIPLE 11

No! Go! Yell! Tell!

NO! GO! YELL! TELL! is a universal, easy-to-remember phrase that applies to virtually every situation regarding your child's safety. Whether it be the site of an accident, a bully or a house on fire, NO! GO! YELL! TELL! applies.

No!

Go!

Yell!

Tell!

DESCRIPTION

NO! Teach your child that it's okay to say "No!" to a person (or a situation) with whom he doesn't feel comfortable.

GO! Teach your child to leave the scene immediately when he feels physically threatened or in danger.

YELL! Teach your child to draw attention to the threatening situation. Teach him to yell "Fire!" rather than "Help!" (Most anything is better than "help.") For example, "There's a stranger after me," "He's not my father" or "This kid is trying to beat me up" are much better than just yelling "Help!"

TELL! Teach your child to tell a safe adult what happened no matter how embarrassing, scary or trivial the incident seems.

NO! GO! YELL! TELL! is a vital tool for your child, especially when it comes to lures. Explain to your child that lures are tricks that people might use to get him to go with them when he knows that he shouldn't. Teach him that a good person knows that it isn't right to do this and would never ask him to come with him.

There are four classic lures. The first lure is the *Bribery Lure*. This is when someone tells your child that he will give him a toy or candy if he comes with him. The second lure is the *Job Lure*. This is when someone offers to pay your child money if he helps him with something. The third lure is the *Assistance Lure*. This is when someone asks your child for help. And the fourth lure is the *Direction Lure*. Do grown-ups ask kids for directions? No.

FAMILY SAFETY PRINCIPLE TOOL 11: Role-play with your child. Pretend to be a stranger using the four lures and have him practice NO! GO! YELL! TELL!

SECTION 4
Why Martial Arts Will Help You Raise a Healthier and Happier Child

The benefits of enrolling your child in a martial arts program extend far beyond self-defense. Martial arts will help your child in nearly every aspect of her life. It will improve your child's health, fitness, athletic abilities, confidence, concentration and behavior.

Does this sound too good to be true? It's not. Many experts agree that martial arts is good medicine for the escalating childhood obesity, increased violence at school and deterioration of the family structure.

There is a reason why Dr. Phil, Jillian Michaels (expert from the television show *The Biggest Loser*), Tony Robbins, pediatricians, child physiologists and educators the world over all recommend martial arts as one of the most valuable activities in which your child can participate.

Confidence   *Composure*

Health   *Control*

Fitness   *Respect*

Strength   *Self-defense*

Flexibility   *Safety*

Endurance   *Success*

Athleticism   *Achievement*

Balance   *Goals*

Peace

DESCRIPTION

Self-Defense
The self-defense benefits of martial arts could be described as *practice the fight so that you don't have to*. As your child trains he will become more confident in his ability to defend himself. As this confidence increases the need to defend himself will decrease naturally because he will begin to carry himself in a more confident manner. He'll project confidence to everyone around him and will be less vulnerable to predatory behavior.

Martial arts training includes strategic or preventative self-defense as well as physical self-defense. Your child will learn how to recognize potentially dangerous situations and how to avoid confrontations.

Athletic Enhancement
There is a reason why every professional sports team in every major sport supplements their training with martial arts. Martial arts training offers several advantages. It is amazingly effective in enhancing general coordination because it uses every part of the body in a balanced way. Upper body, lower body, right side, left side, forward movement, lateral movement and rotational movement are all included in martial arts training.

Fitness
Fitness has three components: strength, flexibility and endurance. Martial arts training demands a balance between the three. Therefore, a child who trains in martial arts will find her weakest areas greatly improved. Because of her greater balance of strength, flexibility and endurance, your child will be less likely to injure herself while participating in other athletic activities.

Health
While martial arts training improves health for people of all ages, it is especially effective for children. It's great exercise and it's fun so kids don't mind doing it. And part of martial arts training includes discussing diet and lifestyle habits so children who grow up training develop healthy habits that stick with them for life.

Concentration
Very few activities engage the mind, body and spirit more than martial arts. Because of this a child's ability to concentrate is greatly enhanced by his martial arts training. He'll bring this ability to concentrate to other activities, too.

Respect and Courtesy
Martial arts techniques are, by nature, designed to injure others when applied. Because of this, martial arts instructors greatly stress the importance of respect, courtesy and restraint. It has been proven time and again that children who are skilled in martial arts tend to be extremely respectful, considerate and composed.

Confidence
Martial arts training always increases a child's confidence for two specific reasons. First, there are no bench sitters. Every child participates and competes against her own potential rather than against the other students. Second, martial arts training is built on the concept of setting your child up for success by giving her a series of realistic, short-term goals that she can attain quickly while keeping her focused on an exciting long-term goal. Each time she experiences success her confidence improves until she begins to believe that she can accomplish just about anything with hard work and dedication.

SECTION 5
School Success Tips

Your child is born with his own set of strengths. Sometimes, these strengths don't always line up with traditional education. We have all seen the really bright kid that can't seem to "get it right" at school or the child who was blessed with great athleticism or a high level of common sense, but who just doesn't seem to be book smart. Regardless of where your child falls in the spectrum there are some simple things you can do to help him establish habits for success at school.

The tough thing will be that not only does your child need to stay on task with these *School Success Tips*, you do, too. Sometimes it might feel like an annoyance when you and your family are having a great time with friends on a school night and have to leave in time to keep your child on schedule with homework and bedtime. Having your child on a schedule means that you have to have one, too.

The benefits far outweigh the inconveniences though. If you follow these eight *School Success Tips* consistently you'll have a happier child and a happier home. Pretty soon you'll be completely invested and excited about following them. It will feel insane not to stick with them. Your child likes to know what to expect. It helps him to feel calm and secure. In fact, you'll feel better, too.

Routine

Habit

Rest

Breakfast

Listen

Example

Consistency

Schedule

Positivity

1. ESTABLISH AND WRITE OUT A DAILY SCHEDULE

There is a lot of power in the written word. It is much easier to get family buy-in when there is a clearly defined schedule posted for everyone to see. Write out a schedule for school days and list the following for your child:

- Time to wake up

- Breakfast time

- What time you need to leave for school

- What time your child will get home from school

- Dinner time

- Homework time

- Bedtime

- And other things that pertain, like feeding the dog, practicing the piano, etc.

Establish this schedule with your child's input (depending on his age and level of maturity). When your child is in on the process he will be a lot more enthusiastic about sticking to it. Then stick to your word and stay on schedule.

It's a challenge to maintain consistency if your child shares his time between two households but it can be done if the adults are willing to communicate and work together. If this is not the case then, at the very least, your child will know what to expect when he comes to stay with you. This will give him added security.

2. ESTABLISH A MORNING ROUTINE

Team up with your child to make a list of everything that she needs to do on school mornings. For example:

- Get dressed

- Feed the cat

- Make lunch

- Do a backpack check
- Etc.

And make sure that your child starts every morning with a healthy breakfast! Like a car, her body needs the proper fuel to perform at peak levels.

3. ATTITUDE IS EVERYTHING

Remember that our children pay much more attention to our actions than they do to our words. If you want your child to have a good attitude about the day you need to have one, too. Remind your child to go to school each day ready to focus, work hard and have fun learning by your example and your words.

4. GREAT HOMEWORK HABITS

Have a designated time and a quiet place for your child to do his homework. Make sure the television is off and there are no disruptions during time. For an older child you might even ask him to hand over his cell phone until he successfully completes his homework.

Encourage your child to do a thorough job and remind him to turn his homework in once he has gone to all the work to do it.

Remember that your child pays closer attention to what you do than to what you say. You lead by your example. A child who is easily distracted might do better if you choose to read or work on your computer doing "your homework," too, during your child's homework time. It often helps to be in the same room with your child doing something quiet.

5. COMMUNICATE WITH YOUR CHILD'S TEACHERS

Your child's teachers can't read your mind. Team up with your child's teachers to get the full picture of how your child is doing at school. Great relationships come from great communication. Ask your child's teachers questions and share concerns.

6. SHARE AT HOME

Ask your child about what she learned at school that day. And then listen. Ask her to tell you about her favorite part of her day. And then listen some more. Give her your full attention and be easily in awe of her achievements.

Do not multitask—text, watch television, etc.—during this time. The time you spend listening to your child is way too valuable to waste. Compliment her for doing a great job telling you about her day, too!

7. ENCOURAGE POSITIVE RELATIONSHIPS

Be highly supportive of your child's friendships with children who have good character and good habits. And gently discourage relationships with kids who have a negative influence. The key word is "gently." This is an exercise in subtlety. Very small signals from you can have very strong influence but if you exert too much force, your child might rebel and withhold information from you.

8. ESTABLISH A BEDTIME ROUTINE

It's so important that your child gets enough rest. A good goal to have is to establish a bedtime routine in which your child goes to bed at a specific time every night. To help your child wind down, incorporate a low-energy activity like reading into the evening before she goes to sleep. Children like routine. They like to know what to expect. Sure, they'll test your boundaries but stick to them. This is for their *School Success*!

SECTION 6
Success In Extracurricular Activities

Whether it be sports, martial arts, music, drama or any other worthwhile extracurricular activity, there are several strategies that you can use to help your child experience success.

Fun

Success

Patience

Variety

DESCRIPTION

WARNING TO DADS: Resist the temptation to live vicariously through your child. We have all seen the dad who pushed his child to excel in something that he wished he had been able to do when he was a kid. This often backfires. The child ends up hating the activity and resenting the parent.

Expose your child to a lot of different activities especially when he is young. Some children like everything. For them the hard part is deciding what not to do. Other children don't seem to like anything. Take heart. If you are patient, something will catch his interest.

Initially, it's okay for your child not to be completely committed to a particular activity. For example, just because he likes soccer doesn't necessarily mean that he wants to practice a lot. Remember, your child thinks it's his "job" to have fun. So if you keep it fun, he'll do a better job. The moment an activity starts to feel like work he'll begin to lose interest (at least most of the time).

A BEAUTIFUL LESSON

I speak from experience. I love martial arts. Not only do I teach it for a living, but it is my extracurricular activity of choice. When my son was born, I could hardly wait until he was old enough to start training. When he was a baby, I'd have my wife bring him to class just to watch. My mom made him a custom karate gi (uniform) when he was two. I was sure he was destined to become a little martial arts superstar.

There was one minor problem, however. My son had absolutely no interest in martial arts. Whenever I brought him to a competition, he preferred to flirt with his babysitter rather than watch.

When he was old enough to train, he did not want to go to class. I forced him. This backfired. Forcing him to take class turned him off to martial arts. He dug in his heels. There is wisdom in the philosophy that excessive punishment only strengthens the need for defiance. Although I didn't feel like I was punishing my son, he did. And he responded accordingly.

Out of frustration, I spoke with a friend of mine whose 14-year old son was excelling at martial arts. He asked me a question that I've never forgotten. He asked, "Do you want your son to be the best 10-year-old martial artist in the area or do you want your son to enjoy the benefits of martial arts for a lifetime?" He told me to lighten up and that my son would be interested if and when he was ready. I've asked countless parents this same question when they come to me concerned about their own children's resistance.

I lightened up. Eventually, he wanted to train in martial arts. Even then I resisted the temptation to push him hard. I had him go to the minimum number of classes each week and didn't even encourage him to practice for quite some time. Now, years later, he loves martial arts and is quite good. But it is not something that this dad made him do. He chose martial arts, made it his own and does it for his own reasons. And I couldn't be happier.

TOOL

When your child finally engages in one or two extracurricular activities, there will come a time (or several times) when he might need a little help to step up his game. When this happens the following guidelines will help you make the process more effective and enjoyable for everyone concerned:

Long-term goals. Encourage your child to set long-term goals. In martial arts training, we encourage children to set the goal of black belt. Regardless of the activity, once your child sets that goal she will be much more likely to achieve it. Having a clear long-term goal will help her navigate through the obstacles that cross her path.

Ample warning. Give your child ample warning before it is time to leave for class or practice. Remember, your child is focused on the present moment. If he's swimming with his friends and you yell out to him that it's time to go to class, he's likely to respond with the classic, "Dad, do I have to go?!" Instead, let your child know well ahead of time so he has ample time to shift gears.

Not optional. Never ask your child if she wants to go to class or practice. You don't ask her if she wants to go to school in the morning. Just like going to school, attending practice or class is part of your not-optional routine. Remind her that she needs to go even if she doesn't feel like it. What often happens is that practice or class ends up being the best time ever and the child doesn't even remember that she resisted going.

Anchor in that enthusiasm. After class or practice, anchor in your child's enthusiasm by asking him questions. Remind him how much fun he had. This is especially valuable if the child complained about not wanting to go to practice that day. The next time he complains about having to go to class, remind him about how much fun he had last time. This strategy works wonders.

Be consistent. Do your best to be consistent about getting your child to class or practice. If she misses a class or practice on occasion, don't worry.

Ask for help. Don't be afraid to ask for help if you feel your child needs it. Sometimes a child might say she wants to quit an activity because she doesn't like it anymore. But the reality is that she feels behind or inadequate in a particular area. As a martial arts teacher, I have been able to re-motivate a child by simply spending a few minutes helping her through a rough spot. Your child's coach or instructor might not be aware that your child is having difficulty until you ask for help. Most will rally and willingly help your child.

Ease into home practice. Many well-intentioned fathers push their children to practice their extracurricular activity too much too soon. Pushing home practice too soon can be counter-productive because it can lead to boredom and burnout. In most cases, it's better to ease your child into the concept of home practice.

Avoid *The Clarinet Syndrome*. The summer before fourth grade, I told my father that I wanted to learn the clarinet. He had a friend who owned a clarinet and wasn't using it. One day, he surprised me with this clarinet. I played it everyday all summer long. Boy, did I have fun!

When the school year started, I began my formal clarinet training. It was pretty fun at first and my teacher said I had potential. He then told my father that I must practice every day for at least half an hour if I was going to be any good. Very quickly the joy left. I no longer wanted to play. Now that I was to practice "officially," the fun was zapped. When I skipped practice, my parents were on me. My dad looked me in the eye on numerous occasions and said, "If you want to be any good at this you need to practice." Well, you know how the story ends. My clarinet career lasted about three months. I call this *The Clarinet Syndrome*.

Keep *The Clarinet Syndrome* from happening in your family. You can gradually step up the time and intensity of home practice but resist the temptation to push too hard too fast. Be consistent. It's best if you can designate specific practice times and stick to them. If your child has the "I'll practice whenever I have time" attitude, she will never have time. Keep practices short. 10–15 minutes is plenty of time and even less is acceptable for beginning students. Over time, as your child matures and his skills improve, you can begin to increase the practice time.

Reward effort. Be as encouraging as possible so that your child will enjoy practice sessions. Your child is more likely to stick to activities in which she feels that she is progressing. Sometimes just noticing an improvement here and there is all it takes to keep her on track.

Don't be too picky. Slowly but surely your child's form will improve. Don't expect too much too soon. Try to find two good things for every correction you make. In most cases, however, leave the correcting to his coach or teacher. You're probably correcting him enough in other areas of his life already.

Make it fun. Making practice fun is the single most important factor in your child's long-term success. You can make it fun by having your child teach you what she is learning. Or make it fun by playing a skill-specific game such as catch, three flies up, H-O-R-S-E, etc. There are many games you can play with your child to help her develop a particular skill. Be creative.

Epilogue

More an art than a science, raising children is both challenging and incredibly rewarding. Each child comes into this world with his own agenda. Oftentimes our children throw curves at us that we never saw coming and, when that happens, it is hard to know exactly what to do.

I'm reminded of a story I once heard about a famous landscape architect ... a master. He traveled the world creating amazing gardens and landscapes at prestigious locations. On days when he felt particularly challenged, he would pull out a mysterious piece of paper from his pocket, glance at it, nod, fold it back up and get to work with renewed inspiration and energy with another masterpiece. People were astounded by his brilliant designs that would seem to appear from thin air after he studied that piece of paper.

Eventually, the master died. His curious colleagues approached his widow and asked to see that mysterious piece of paper as they were convinced it contained the secret to his success.

After much to-do, she allowed them one glance at the old slip of paper. As they gathered around, she carefully unfolded the paper. They looked at the writing. It simply said, "When laying sod, always put the green side up."

I love this story! It reminds me how easy it is to overcomplicate things, especially parenting. In my experience, the answers to most parenting challenges are in the *Parenting Guidelines* at the beginning of this book. We only have to remember to call upon them in times of need.

I hope you'll find A DAD'S TOOLBOX FOR BETTER PARENTING to be a valuable resource for years to come.

Happy parenting!

A Dad's Toolbox for Better Parenting

Notes

Notes

Made in the USA
San Bernardino, CA
07 June 2018